BY YOUR SIDE

BY YOUR SIDE

How the Spirits Can Help You
Every Day

Colin Fry

WINDSOR
PARAGON

First published 2010
by Rider, an imprint of Ebury Publishing
This Large Print edition published 2013
by AudioGO Ltd
by arrangement with
Ebury Publishing

Hardcover   ISBN: 978 1 4713 5711 4
Softcover   ISBN: 978 1 4713 5712 1

British Library Cataloguing in Publication Data available

Printed and bound in Great Britain by TJ International Limited

I would like to dedicate this book to, as always, my partner Mikey and my manager Eden, who through thick and thin have been 'always by my side'.

CONTENTS

INTRODUCTION

The Spirit Network

> 'There is an infinite storehouse of knowledge which is placed at the disposal of all who desire to have it, but it must be earned by growth and struggle, by evolution and progress.' SILVER BIRCH THROUGH THE MEDIUMSHIP OF MAURICE BARBANELL

During the course of my career as a medium I have communicated with a multitude of spirits. I have connected with people who have passed over to the other side from all walks of life, all cultures and parts of the world, and from different generations stretching back hundreds of years. They have passed on to me an incredible range of messages, from simple affirmations of their love for those they have left behind to important advice about events that are unfolding—or sometimes about to unfold—in this earthly life. As they have done this they have also communicated to me a broader message: they are there for us, always.

Today, we live in the age of the internet. We are most of us connected to each other and can communicate instantly by text and email or through social networking sites like Facebook, Bebo, Twitter and the rest. It struck me quite recently that, in a way, the universe that lies on the other side of this life is a little like this. It is, if you like, the spirit worldwide web, a vast network of connections, waiting to be accessed at all times. It can provide all the things that the collection of websites, friends, contacts, confidants, advisers and family members provide us with in this life. It can help us deal with difficulties relating to love, faith, money, work, relationships, loss and lots more. It can offer us advice, lend us insight, help us right wrongs and even make us smile. It can also show us the way ahead in our lives both in the short and long term.

This book is a collection of some of the more memorable and remarkable encounters I've had with the other side during my lifetime as a medium. It shows how communications can come from the most unexpected quarters at the most unlikely of times. It also illustrates the amazing range of ways in which the spirit world works for each of us by providing hope, inspiration, support, guidance, love, friend-ship, knowledge and much more besides.

The spirit world really is around us all the time, always watching over us, always working for us. By the end of this book I hope you will appreciate that help is close at hand, that there is always someone by your side.

'Voices All Around You'

The journey that led me to becoming a medium was a long and eventful one. It has taken me many years to learn how to channel and interpret the thoughts of those who have left the earthly plane and passed over to the other side. There were times when I found it hard, some occasions when I almost felt like giving up. But the more I developed my gift, the more I understood the true importance and profound potential of communicating with the spirit world. Most of all, I began to see that it has the power to help, guide, support and inspire us all.

I had been aware of the spirit dimension since I was a young boy. From an early age I was conscious of being in the presence of those who had passed over. I often glimpsed spirits. To be honest, I imagined they were just a part of my own little world. I was thinking as a child, of course. I couldn't see the broader picture. It was only in my teens that I began to truly understand the significance of what I was feeling and seeing. It was then that I began to communicate with and learn from them. As I did so I began to realise that—just like the earthly world that was opening up to me at the time—the spirit world was a much bigger, much more sophisticated and complicated place than I'd imagined. It was also a world filled with possibilities.

The enlightenment that I experienced during this period owed a great deal to the remarkable people I met along the way. There's no question in my mind, I would not have become the medium I am today if it hadn't been for them.

I had many memorable psychic experiences when I was young, some of which changed my view of not just this world but the next one too. None was more important in moulding me as a young medium than the one I had at the Dome in Brighton back in the late 1970s.

I had grown up in Sussex and had a number of friends who worked in Brighton. A couple of them worked at the city's famous Regency landmark, the Dome. They knew about my interest in spiritualism and mediumship so when the best-known medium in Britain—and perhaps the world—at the time, Doris Stokes, came to demonstrate there, they asked me whether I wanted to come along.

I jumped at the chance. I went with a few friends who shared my interest in spiritualism and mediumship.

Doris Stokes was, of course, the subject of a lot of criticism and controversy during her life, all of it grossly unfair as far as I am concerned. To my mind she was quite simply one of the most brilliant mediums—and amazing women—of her time. She was, as I discovered that night, a lovely person too.

She gave an outstanding demonstration that night. I had seen one or two mediums within the spiritualist movement but this was on a different scale and level of communication altogether. You could have heard a pin drop within the Dome that night. The hundreds of people packed in the auditorium were, almost literally, spellbound by Doris's ability to connect and communicate with the spirit world.

It was as we were leaving the auditorium that, to my delight—and slight terror—one of the friends who worked at the Dome asked me if I would like to go backstage to meet Doris.

'Yes, I'd love to,' I said, rather nervously.

Only one of the friends who'd accompanied me to the demonstration had the nerve to come with me. The rest stayed in the foyer.

Along with my friend I was ushered into the rear of the theatre and towards the main dressing rooms. We were greeted initially by Doris's husband John. He was extremely friendly. He asked us how we'd enjoyed the show and took a real interest in who we were and where we'd come from. He then began leading us into his wife's dressing room.

I will never forget what happened next.

I can still see her now. Doris was sitting at her dressing table, quietly sipping a well-deserved post-show cup of tea. She was, just as she was on stage, the most down-to-earth, ordinary-looking lady you're ever likely to meet. She was a true star but there were none of the trappings of stardom about her.

She would have been quite within her rights to be a bit cheesed off at being disturbed. She was an elderly lady by now and was probably exhausted from the show. But if she was tired she didn't show it. She seemed genuinely pleased to have company.

My friend and I shuffled into the small dressing room, not quite sure where to stand. Almost immediately Doris got up from her chair and made a beeline for me, totally ignoring my friend.

'Oh hello, dear,' she said, extending her hand and beaming her full, fifty-megawatt smile. 'My guide is telling me that you've got the gift.'

I had read a lot about Doris and knew that she had a spirit guide called Romanoff. She didn't identify the person talking to her as him, but I got the feeling it was him. I really didn't know what to say and stood there looking rather bemused, I'm sure.

'He's telling me that voices are going to happen all around you. And, darling, you will travel the world. You will travel the world and you will write books and go on television,' she said, before reeling off a list of countries that she said I would visit.

To be honest, at that point I thought she was

being deliberately dramatic, putting on a show for her guests. She was saying that I was going to go on tour in Australia, New Zealand and Japan, for goodness' sake. Inside I was thinking: 'Yeah right, of course I am.'

Perhaps she sensed my disbelief because she then began to look slightly over my shoulder. 'Darling, there's a man standing next to you,' she said. 'He's quite short and there's something wrong with his back.'

It was as if an electric shock had gone through me—I sensed who it was immediately. She was talking about my late grandfather Laurie. He'd come to see me on the night he passed away, when I was ten years old. In the years that followed I had seen, felt or heard him often. He had been a guiding spirit, offering me advice and reassurance as I passed through the difficult teenage years of my life. I wasn't surprised that Doris had seen him standing alongside me. I felt his presence with me a lot.

'Did your grandfather have a deformed back?' Doris asked me.

'He had a humpback.'

'I can also see a shadow over his eye.'

'He was blind in one eye.'

Within moments she'd told me his name and explained that he was someone I saw often. 'Oh, that's nice. He's telling me that he has been with you ever since he passed over,' she said, smiling.

Soon after that, Doris turned away and headed back to her chair. John asked us if we minded leaving now. 'It's getting late and Doris needs her rest,' he explained.

I left the dressing room in quite an emotional

state. It felt like one of the most momentous things that had ever happened to me.

I'd not spoken much about my granddad to anyone, despite the fact I'd been seeing him for the best part of seven years by now. To have another medium actually confirm everything that I'd experienced was overwhelming. I'd had my doubts about what I'd seen and felt in Laurie's presence. Now a medium—and not just any medium—had validated all that had happened.

I left the theatre in a state of euphoria. For the next few days I'm sure I walked around with a great big grin on my face.

It was in the days, months and years which followed that the real significance of what Doris had said to me began to sink in, however. On a basic level, that brief encounter opened my eyes and my mind to aspects of the spirit world that I'd never thought of until then. For instance, I know it sounds rather silly now, but until that point I'd assumed that messages always came from people you knew.

I was only just starting to demonstrate my own mediumship, but I had had encounters with spirits that I didn't recognise. For example, since I was young I'd seen an elderly man sitting at the bottom of my bed. He was very different from my grandfather, older and from another era, probably the Victorian era. But I assumed he was just some stranger. I hadn't really engaged him in a meaningful conversation in the way that I had spoken with my grandfather. It hadn't occurred to me that there might be other people, other strangers, watching over me, with knowledge about who I was, what I was doing with my life—and most amazingly of all—where I was heading in the future.

And as time has gone on the importance of that meeting with Doris has grown rather than diminished. In the thirty or so years since I met Doris her reading has proved more accurate than I could ever have imagined.

A few years ago, for instance, when I went to New Zealand to give demonstrations for the first time, I suddenly heard her voice in my head. I was walking down the street in the city of Hamilton when Doris started reciting the list of countries that she said I'd one day visit, just as she had that night at the Dome. Among the places that she'd listed had been countries like Japan, Sweden and Australia. But what suddenly struck me was that she hadn't just got the places right—she'd got them in the exact order that I had visited them.

She had also been right about me appearing on television and writing books. Most importantly of all, of course, she had been absolutely right about the fact that 'voices are going to happen all around you'.

Those voices fill the pages of this book. I hope they echo as powerfully and inspirationally for you as they did for me.

HOW THE SPIRITS CAN BRING YOU HOPE

'Die happily and look forward to taking up a
new and better form. Like the sun, only when
you set in the west can you rise in the east.'
JELALUDDIN RUMI

I often end my public demonstrations with the same
thought. I make no apology for doing so. It is the
most important message I can possibly share with my
audiences. And it is this:

Death is the biggest lie that we are told. It
isn't the end, existence doesn't finish when we
draw our last breath. Life continues
elsewhere, in an afterlife; when we leave this
earthly plane we pass over into the spirit
dimension.

As a medium, I spend my day-to-day life
experiencing the amazing reality behind this
message. I work closely with those who have the
most personal knowledge of its truth: the spirits who
have passed over to the other side. As I do so, I am
able to give people one of the most precious and
powerful commodities in this life—hope.

The spirit world never ceases to fascinate and
surprise me. During the thirty years or so that I
have being working as a medium, I have seen it at
work in a myriad different ways. It is forever
spreading hope. I'd like to begin this book with

some stories that illustrate how.

The Red Carpet

One of the things I was told early on during my development as a medium was this: 'There will be times when you will think you want to give up—but you never will.'

I don't think there's ever been a truer word spoken.

There have actually been several times in my career when I've felt like turning my back on the spirit world. On one or two occasions I have, in my own mind at least, drawn a veil over the whole thing. But the spirit world has ensured that I have always been drawn back.

The most striking example of this happened during my late twenties. In the wake of my encounter with Doris Stokes I spent a lot of time developing my mediumship during my teens and early twenties. But then during my mid twenties, I got to a point where to all intents and purposes I'd given up. I would do the occasional reading for people and attend a Church meeting every now and again, but in general I was getting to the point where I was thinking, 'This is going nowhere'.

The fact that I was doing well in my chosen career in retail management was driving me even further in a different direction. My mediumship was, more and more, being put on the back burner. To a large degree this was because I felt I'd hit a buffer. At the back of my mind I had this nagging feeling that I was supposed to be doing more with my gift. But I didn't know what.

I kept putting the thought out to the spirit world

that 'there must be more to this, but what is it? What am I supposed to be doing?' Every time I did that I would get a single word answer. Every time they would say, 'Wait.'

This went on for eighteen months. 'Wait, wait, wait.' I felt so frustrated. 'What am I waiting for?' I started to say to myself. 'And is it actually worth the wait?'

So by my mid twenties the inevitable had happened. I had reached a point where I decided I was going to give it all up. I knew I'd always be interested in the subject, but only as a hobby. Instead I'd concentrate on my career and friends and relationships. Of course, I should have realised that the spirit world would have other ideas. As ever, they were close by and they were soon intervening.

I was a manager at a carpet warehouse at the time. One day an elderly couple came in looking for a carpet for their flat in Hove. The lady was in a wheelchair. To be honest, I was impatient to get away from them. I sensed immediately that they were the type of customers who would look around but never actually commit to buying anything.

They were looking for a red carpet. I must have shown them every single sample of red carpet we had in the warehouse, and there were a lot of red carpets there, let me tell you. In the end, they eventually came down to a choice between two carpets. By now I was pretty confident they were going to buy one of them after all so I agreed to go along to their flat the next day to measure it up and give them a quote.

In the past I have briefly mentioned the story of what happened when I returned to visit the couple.

3

But I have always held back from describing what happened that day—and subsequently—in full detail. I do so now because it was, in many ways, one of the most moving and powerful displays of the spirit world at work I have ever been involved in. It illustrates the point I am making in this chapter, and this book, perfectly.

The following morning I went along to the address they'd given me where I was greeted by the husband. He took me through to their front lounge where they wanted the carpet fitted. I put my briefcase down, took out my tape measure and notebook and started taking measurements.

As I did so the most vivid spirit voice was suddenly talking to me. 'Tell this man that you know he uses this room for séances,' it said.

I ignored it and carried on. But in my head the voice kept repeating itself and as it did so it got louder and louder and louder. 'Tell him that you know he uses this room for séances!'

Eventually I thought to myself: 'I've got to ask him, otherwise this is never going to stop.'

So I turned to the gentleman, smiled politely and said: 'I have to ask this, sir—and I'm terribly sorry if I offend you or your wife in any way and I will leave your home immediately if I do—but you use this room for séances, don't you?'

He didn't bat an eyelid and replied immediately. 'Yes,' he said. 'And how do you know that?'

'Because a spirit voice just told me,' I said.

With that he grabbed me by the arm and rushed me back into the kitchen where his wife was sitting having a cup of tea. 'Tell my wife what you've just said.'

When I did she smiled. 'Oh yes, my dear,' she

4

said. 'We knew you'd be coming.'

I was a bit chippy at the time so I said: 'Of course you did, we made an appointment for me to measure up for a new carpet.'

But she ignored my juvenile humour and said, 'No, we knew you'd be coming for another reason. Do you know what a physical phenomenon circle is?'

'Yes, I do,' I said. 'It's where a group of people communicate directly with the spirit world and a spirit even makes use of their own voice through the medium. They used to happen in the old days but they don't exist any more.'

'Oh yes they do,' she said. 'We've run one now for more than twenty years.'

She went on to explain that the circle had been formed by her husband's mother who had been a very successful medium. She had passed over now, but they had continued to meet once a month when a trance medium would come down from the north of England to sit with them.

'Back in November the trance medium who sat with us brought through a spirit which told us that in the month of May, just before his birthday, a young man would come to us through the course of his work and he would identify himself as a medium,' she said. 'He told us that the spirit world wanted us to take on the responsibility of developing him. They had big plans for him.'

Even I was taken aback. The thing that hit me most was that it was May and it was two days before my birthday. It was an echo of what Doris Stokes had said to me a decade or so earlier. Again there was the promise of me travelling the world practising mediumship.

5

After a while I composed myself. This was silly, I said to myself.

'We sit on Tuesday evenings. Would you like to come and join us?' the man asked.

More out of politeness than anything else, I said, 'Yes, OK.'

I left the house feeling a mixture of emotions. I was intrigued but also I was still more than a little sceptical. How could this humble couple living in a flat in Hove hold the key to the rest of my life? How did I know that it was going to come to anything? Doris Stokes' predictions hadn't come true. Why should these people's projections be any different?

When I went back the following Tuesday I still felt this dilemma. Was this really the big breakthrough I needed? Or was it another blind alley? Did I even want any of this?

The couple, whom I now knew as Geraldine and John, were pleased to see me. They were lovely people and there was another guy there, an old chap called Lennie who was a local barber. John explained that they'd had a number of sitters over the years but that it had been hard to keep them coming consistently.

We all filed into a little dark room and sat down. We then sang to raise the energies. I knew about physical phenomena circles so there was nothing particularly unusual about this. I'd read a lot about them.

We sat for an hour and to my mind nothing happened. No one said very much.

'That went well,' John said afterwards.

'Did it?' I thought.

'Will you come back next Tuesday?'

'OK,' I said, although I wasn't sure.

I was growing to like John and Geraldine so I didn't want to let them down. I went back the following week and we started the same way as before, singing, the lights down. But then something strange happened. I suddenly felt my eyes going, as if I was falling asleep.

At first I put it down to tiredness. I'd had a busy day at work and it was quite warm in the room. 'Mustn't fall asleep,' I told myself, but it was too late. Before I knew it I'd nodded off. I'd gone out like a light.

What seemed like a few moments later I was sitting in the room with the lights on. I was mortified. 'I'm so sorry I dozed off,' I said.

'Don't worry about it now,' John said. 'I'll close the circle.'

A few moments later we were all in the kitchen having a cup of tea. I was still feeling terrible. They were such a nice couple, and I thought I'd really offended them. I couldn't stop apologising. 'Sorry, I had a busy day at work and it was quite hot in there. I'm really sorry I nodded off,' I said.

It was then that I noticed that the wife, Geraldine, was quietly crying. Now I felt really bad. This circle obviously meant a lot to them. I hadn't taken it seriously. I'd upset them. I wanted the ground to open up and swallow me. 'I am so sorry,' I started to say before John cut me short.

'You've got no idea what happened, have you?' he said.

'What do you mean?'

'Colin, sit down. You didn't fall asleep—you fell into a trance.'

'I couldn't have,' I said. 'I'd remember it.'

7

'No, you wouldn't,' John said. 'Trance mediums have no idea what is being channelled through them and retain no memory of what they say while they are connected to the spirit world.'

'Really,' I said, slightly lost for words.

John looked across at Geraldine who was still dabbing her face with a handkerchief. 'Colin, the reason Geraldine is so emotional is that while you were in the trance our son communicated through you.'

I was too stunned to even speak for a second. 'Your son,' I said eventually.

'Yes, Geraldine and I have a son who was killed in a train crash when he was young, only in his teens. He'd been going up to London to see a show in the West End. I'd advised him to get on the front of the train so that he could make a quick getaway when he reached London. The train had ploughed into another train head on. The people at the rear of the train survived but those at the front didn't,' he said.

John didn't need to explain to me how that had affected him. I could see in his eyes that it haunted him still.

'We have been trying to reach him for years through various mediums. But tonight, while you were in a trance he came through and spoke to us through you,' John said.

I was overwhelmed.

By now Geraldine had stopped crying. She took my hand and smiled at me. 'We knew you were meant to be a part of our circle,' she said. 'Tonight you proved it.'

I stayed and chatted with them for a while that evening. They told me how the loss of their son had shattered their lives completely. They had both been quite religious people and had taken part in spiritualist meetings and had sat in circles for years. But, like so many people, they lost their faith when they lost their son. They hadn't been able to understand how God could have done that to them, how He could have been so cruel. They had, for a long time, turned their back on the Church and the spirit world, although I found out much later that an encounter with the famous medium Leslie Flint had started them back on the path of spirit communication.

'You've given us hope again. Now we'd like to help you discover your true gift by giving you the chance to develop your mediumship in a regular circle.'

It was the beginning of one of the most significant and long-lasting relationships of my life.

Looking back now, I can see quite clearly that those twenty-four hours were among the most important of my life. It was in John and Geraldine's circle that I began to develop my trance and physical mediumship. The knowledge I developed there allowed me to become a demonstrating medium, eventually appearing on television and on stage around the world. Just as they'd predicted.

As I did so I found myself able to deliver many more messages of hope. Few were quite as profound or as moving as that one, however.

'The day which we fear as our last is but the birth into eternity.' SENECA

A Knock On The Door

I am always humbled by the time, effort and trouble that some people take in order to visit me for a private con sultation or to see me demonstrating live. Over the years, I have been visited by people from all over the world. I've had private clients come to see me from as far afield as Australia and New Zealand, Japan and the USA. I've been visited by Indian holy men, Arab and European royalty, celebrities and city businessmen. Whether they are the highest or the humblest, I have always done my level best to help them and many of them have been people who have left a lasting impression on me.

One of the most powerful and emotional readings I ever gave was for a lady who travelled 10,000 miles to see me, from Brazil. She was a lovely gentle lady and her name was Maria. She wasn't actually Brazilian, she was German by birth, but she had moved to the Brazilian city of Sao Paulo with her husband who had been given a posting there. They had loved the country and decided to stay permanently. Having visited Brazil myself, I can understand why. It's a fabulous place.

It was clear from Maria's demeanour, however, that she wasn't happy. Outwardly she appeared a vibrant and warm woman. She was well dressed and intelligent. I got the impression that, in material terms, life had been good to her. And yet she looked like someone for whom something was missing. I sensed there was a hole in her life. It soon became apparent what it was.

Maria was a young woman; she was twenty-six or twenty-seven years old. As we sat down and the reading began, I connected with an elderly man. I

10

quickly identified him as her grandfather. The first thing I was aware of was the heavy accent with which he spoke.

'If I had met this man in life I wouldn't have been able to understand him,' I said to her. 'He spoke with a German accent but it was an unusual German accent.'

She laughed at this.

'I'm going to have to trust my instincts here,' I said. 'I believe your grandfather was Polish but lived most of his adult life in Germany. But he'd never lost his Polish accent.'

'Yes, you are absolutely right,' she said.

I sensed that she was worried that I might have trouble interpreting what he was saying so I reassured her. 'Don't worry. Fortunately everything comes through to me on the vibration of thought so I'll be able to understand him,' I explained.

The grandfather started to show me that he wasn't alone on the other side, far from it. He began to relate to me the fact that he was surrounded by four children. 'They are here with me now,' he said.

This produced an almost immediate reaction from Maria. She began crying. 'They are my children,' she said quietly.

As the connection continued the man showed me that two of these children had never been born into this world. They had been miscarried.

She nodded at this. 'Yes, that's right,' she confirmed.

'The other two survived for a very short time,' I said.

'Yes,' she replied, by now crying almost

uncontrollably. The communication became very emotional, both for me and for her.

'Your grandfather is showing me that you cannot have another child,' I said.

She simply shook her head.

'He is showing me that during your fourth labour there was a complication,' I said.

'Yes,' she said.

'As a consequence they had to perform an emergency hysterectomy.'

My heart really went out to Maria. She was a young woman who should have had many child-bearing years ahead of her. Life can seem so cruel at times. Not only had she lost four children, she had also had the opportunity to have children taken away from her. She was clearly devastated by this.

As the reading drew to a close and the presence of her grandfather began to fade, I felt one last thought being communicated to me. I was careful about how to phrase it. I didn't want it to upset her.

'Your grandfather is putting through a very specific thought to me,' I said. 'He is saying to me that you will get a child.'

As I'd feared this did upset her.

'I'm sorry, Colin, I can't accept that. I thought you understood I can't have a child after what happened,' she said.

I understood her anguish, but I had to explain the message. 'He didn't say have a child, he said *get* a child,' I said.

She looked at me doubtfully. In truth I don't think either of us quite understood what it meant.

Despite the high emotion of the hour or so that

we spent together, Maria was genuinely pleased with the sitting. She told me that she and her husband had accepted that they wouldn't share their life with a child. I could see in her eyes that even though she'd accepted her situation there was nonetheless a great sadness in it.

So, in the absence of any children in this life, she'd come to find some evidence that the children she'd lost were still in existence. To her immense happiness she'd been given that.

Maria told me that she'd stay in touch when she got back to Brazil. To be honest, many people say that and never do stay in touch. I don't blame them. Often my job is to help them move on with their lives and they don't have the time or the inclination to look back. So I thought no more about it.

It was about two months later that I received a letter with a Brazilian postmark on it. 'Dear Colin, I'm sorry it's taken me so long to reply to thank you for my sitting,' it began. 'But some very strange events have unfolded since I returned to Brazil.'

Maria went on to describe what had happened since she'd flown back from England. She had returned to her life with her husband in Sao Paulo. 'I told my husband that the sitting had gone well. I didn't tell him any details about it. Then one morning we were sitting having breakfast and there was a knock on the door,' she wrote. 'There was a nun standing at the door which we found odd because neither of us had much to do with the church any more. We'd lost a lot of our faith after losing so many children.'

She went on: 'The nun explained that she was from a nearby convent and a baby boy had been put into their care. She wanted to know whether my husband and I would consider adopting the boy.'

Maria admitted that she and her husband had never even considered trying to adopt. They hadn't registered with an agency or even talked about it with friends or neighbours so she was at a loss to explain why the nun had come to their door.

She concluded that it must have been because, in local terms, they were relatively well-off. The child was con sidered quite special and the nuns didn't want to place him in the state orphanage.

'My husband and I thought about it that day and spoke again in the evening. It was amazing. We both decided there and then that we should go ahead and adopt the boy. Within a few weeks we had welcomed him into our home. He is sleeping in a cot a few feet away from where I am writing this letter to you at this very minute,' she said.

She concluded by thanking me again for the reading. She said that it had helped her move on with her life, and no sooner had she done so than she was rewarded with a miracle: a baby that she could finally raise and call her own.

'It seems my grandfather's prediction came true,' she said. 'I have a baby at last. Colin, I can't thank you enough for what you have done.'

I've received many hundreds of letters over the years. Many of them have been very moving, many of them extremely gratifying. I don't think I've ever received a letter that made me feel so genuinely and deeply pleased for someone else.

I shed a little tear, I must admit.

Maria's experience illustrated perfectly how the spirit world is at work around us all the time. She

14

and her husband had resigned themselves to the fact that because they couldn't conceive a baby they would have to live a life without children.

Yet the powers-that-be had decided that Maria was going to have a child. It showed how omnipresent—and resourceful—the spirit world can be. And how determined it is that we should never give up hope . . .

SPIRIT SECRET
The great thing about developing a relationship with the spirit world is that there is no absolute way that anyone can tell you how to do it. It's personal.

So when someone says: 'My mum comes and talks to me every night and it's lovely,' and the cynics and the sceptics say: 'Oh they've lost the plot,' I say: 'That's great, I'm really happy for you.'

If a bereaved parent comes to me and asks me whether I think their son or daughter is sending them signs I say: 'It doesn't matter what I think, it's what you think that's important. If you feel that's what's happening, then that's what's happening.'

Because it's personal.

A Fateful Decision

'The day on which one starts out is not the time to start one's preparations.'
TRADITIONAL SAYING FROM NIGERIA

The spirit world can help guide and advise us in this

15

life, but ultimately the decisions we take must be ours and ours alone. Sometimes those decisions are incredibly difficult, and that was never truer than in the case of a gentleman for whom I did a reading a few years ago.

When he'd made the booking over the phone, I'd made a mental note to myself that his name and his voice sounded African. Sure enough, when he arrived he introduced himself as a diplomat for the government of a central African country. I can't name the country for reasons that will become apparent.

I liked him immediately. He was a very charismatic, imposing figure, a distinguished-looking and highly educated man. He was also one of those people who have a wonderful honesty about themselves.

The mood was very light and friendly as we began the reading. But that soon changed.

He had brought with him a bulky, official-looking briefcase, the kind that government ministers here carry around with them. Once we'd sat down, he placed the briefcase on the coffee table, flicked open the catches and withdrew a large brown envelope.

I could see immediately that this was an important envelope. It was stamped quite clearly with a government seal 'For Your Eyes Only'.

'Oh crikey, what am I getting involved in here?' I said to myself.

He slid it over to me. 'I regret you can't open this envelope. But I'd like you to hold it and tell me what you feel,' he said.

No sooner had he placed the envelope in my hands than I began to sense a strong, male

16

presence in the room. I quickly identified him as the man's father. 'I have your father with me,' I said, which seemed to surprise him.

So as to establish his identity properly, I told him about some memories his father was relaying to me from his boyhood.

I remember it was about an idyllic day the two of them had once spent together, skimming stones on a lake. His father had been a very hard-working man who had pushed himself to the limits to support his family. He said he remembered it as one day of fun they'd had together during his childhood.

The man seemed very moved by this.

'Do you understand this?' I asked.

'Yes, I certainly do,' he said.

Father and son were obviously close. As the image of the two figures standing at the edge of the lake faded, his father's tone changed. He became quite anxious; there was a sudden urgency in his voice. I took a moment to digest what he was telling me; it was clearly very important.

'Your father is telling me that under no circumstances must you go home,' I said after a while.

The man simply smiled. 'I thought that he would say that,' he replied. 'But unfortunately I have to go home because if I don't they will kill my family.'

What he said stunned me. For a moment or two I didn't know what to say. It was clear that I couldn't—and probably shouldn't—ask any more questions.

Soon afterwards the reading drew to a close. I shook hands with him and wished him all the best. I couldn't resist asking whether he was going back to Africa soon.

He sighed. 'Yes, I will go back next week,' he said.

The following week I was in the kitchen listening to the news on the radio. My ears pricked up when I heard the name of the same African country. To my horror I then listened as the newsreader described reports of an assassination there. A man, a leading diplomat, had been killed only twenty-four hours after arriving back in the country from the UK.

I froze, then waited for the name, even though I knew already it had to be the same man.

Sure enough it was.

For a few days afterwards it bothered me terribly. I kept thinking about the envelope. What was inside it? Had its contents been the cause of his assassination? Strangely, I later had a dream that he'd taken the envelope back home with him but that when his bosses opened it they found it was empty.

As I mulled it over I came to the conclusion that he must have been thinking about passing on information to a Western government. I don't think he was a spy. But I think he was sufficiently concerned about the contents of the envelope to feel he had a moral responsibility to make it known. I got the feeling that the authorities back in his country had told him that if he didn't return with the documentation he would have to consider the safety of his family.

But that still didn't answer the question of why he had come to see me? Why had he sought out his father, especially if he was going to ignore his advice?

As the days wore on I got a clear feeling that he had known his family would be safe if he went back home, but that he would be killed. On the other hand, if he stayed here and passed on the documents, he would be safe but his family would be killed. He had decided to sacrifice himself to save his family. So he had come to me looking for some evidence of the afterlife.

At the darkest hour in his life, he needed some hope for the future. It was going to make it easier for him to sacrifice his own life if he had some evidence that his existence would go on. His father coming through gave him the confirmation.

Deep down I kept thinking, should I have done more to stop him going back? But eventually I realised it wasn't my responsibility. My job was to deliver the message, which I did. It was then up to him to make the decision whether he went back or not. He had been an incredibly brave man—and he had done what he felt he had to do in order to protect his family. I couldn't have stopped him from doing that—nor should I have.

My only consolation was that I'd given him confirmation of the spirit world's existence—and perhaps the hope he needed in order to go back home to meet his fate.

2.

HOW THE SPIRITS CAN BRING
YOU PEACE

'Life is always a polarity. If there were no
darkness there would be no light. If there
were no trouble there could never be any
peace. If the sun always shone you would not
appreciate it. You have to learn sometimes
through conditions that seem a nuisance. One
day you will look back and say, "We learned
our best lessons not when the sun was shining,
but when the storm was at its greatest, when
the thunder roared, the lightning flashed, the
clouds obscured the sun and all seemed dark
and hopeless." ' SILVER BIRCH

One of the most common things people are in search
of when they come to me as a medium is forgiveness.
A phrase I hear all the time is: 'I wish we'd patched
up our differences when they were still alive.'
Experience has taught me that forgiveness
can—and does—happen on the other side. It's a
piece of knowledge that has brought many people
peace, including me.

A Victorian Gentleman

When I was a little boy I always used to tell my mum
that there was an old man who often stood at the
bottom of my bed and who looked like Dr Who. This
was when I was very little, at the start of the 1960s, so

Dr Who at that time was the late, great William Hartnell, the first Doctor. He had long white hair that went down to his shoulders. This old man's hair was just like that.

He wasn't a menacing presence in any way. Quite the opposite, in fact. He used to smile at me. I got the real sense that he was my friend.

After a while, he began to speak to me, passing on little pearls of wisdom or simply talking to me about my day-to-day life. I found him very easy to speak to, as if I knew him, even though, clearly, I didn't.

I had learned at a young age that I had to be careful when I talked to other people about the spirits I saw. I'd mentioned the things I'd seen a few times and been chastised for it. Occasionally, however, I'd be unable to resist repeating something the grey-haired figure had told me. Whenever I did so my mother would shoot me a look that might have turned me to marble.

'Where did you hear that?' she'd demand.

'The old man told me,' I'd say.

She'd simply shake her head and tell me to think carefully before repeating such things. No matter what she said, however, she couldn't keep the old man away.

And when I started to develop my mediumship as a young man, he became more and more of an influence. In fact, along with my grandfather, he became probably the most influential spirit connection of my life.

It was when I began working as a trance medium that his identity was revealed to me. It turned out he was my main spirit guide.

I remember when people first started telling me

about guides, I thought it was a bit fanciful, a bit airy-fairy. Everyone seemed to have Native American Indians or nuns guiding them. I had a few that seemed to emerge early on but mine seemed to be ordinary people. One was a doctor and another a schoolteacher, although I also had one strange one who was a Chinese alchemist. But the most regular one was the grey-haired man.

When I joined my development circle with my friends John and Geraldine in Hove, it was his voice and his words that tended to speak most often when I went into a trance.

At first he didn't tell me his name but eventually, after I'd spoken his words many times, he revealed it was Magnus. He was reluctant to say more than this. He said it was only part of his earthly name.

As the years rolled on he revealed little bits of his life. At one stage he told me that he had been the director of a publishing company in London. His offices had been based around Bloomsbury, the centre of the book trade in the Victorian era.

On another occasion he revealed that he had been born in Edinburgh. Unusually for the time, his parents had separated, their marriage was dissolved and his mother took him back to her home, the city of London. He left Edinburgh at the age of eighteen months and never saw the city again.

As I became more experienced as a medium, I was able to connect with his spirit more and more easily. I often found myself in conversation with him. I would feel his presence around me virtually all the time. It was almost as if he was my shadow.

As we became closer I began to learn a lot more

about him. And as I did so, I learned more about the spirit world that he inhabited and how it worked.

The most revealing conversation we had concerned something that had happened to him when he was in his middle age. It was clear he still regretted it, even now on the other side of life. It had only been on the spirit side of life that he saw the consequences of what he'd done.

During his earthly existence Magnus had been a wealthy man and had a large family with a number of children. Unfortunately, as was so often the case in the nineteenth century, several of his children had passed over before him.

One of his sons, the eldest of his children, Valentine, has also communicated through me. He confirmed that Magnus's children, and indeed his wife, had actually been quite frightened of him when he was alive. This tied in with something that Magnus had said to me about how his children had despised him.

His family's fear of him wasn't helped by the fact that he wasn't a well-tempered man. He struggled with his business at times and he would come home from his office in a terrible temper some days. It was on one of these days that something happened which would come to haunt Magnus to eternity.

One afternoon he came home from the office early and walked into his drawing room to find a maid still cleaning the fireplace. She clearly hadn't been expecting him back home so early. When Magnus stormed into the drawing room and slammed the door after him she was so frightened she jumped in the air. As she did so she hit the fire with her poker, sending an ember flying out of the fire and on to the ornate Persian rug that lay next to the hearth. To the girl's horror the ember had immediately scorched the carpet, leaving a terrible black mark.

Magnus flew into an instant rage and started screaming at her. He then summoned the butler and ordered that this young maid be sacked and thrown out of the house immediately.

He admitted to me that he just did it instinctively. Afterwards he didn't give it another thought. He never saw the girl again, nor did he ever think about her again. Until he passed over, that is.

Magnus has taught me so much about the spirit world and how it operates. It was he who first explained to me what happens when a soul passes over from this earthly existence into the spirit world. Each new arrival undergoes a life review, the results of which will influence the type of existence to be experienced on the other side.

It was during his life review that Magnus was shown the consequences of what he'd done on the spur of the moment in his drawing room that day.

This particular girl had been only fourteen years old. Because she'd left Magnus's employment in such a hurry she had no reference, no severance payment. Nothing. As a result she'd been forced to wander the streets with no money. After a few days she'd ended up sleeping rough behind packing crates in Whitechapel.

During his life review Magnus was shown how she had lain there for a couple of nights and then died of the cold and hunger. Such were the terrible conditions of the streets in the East End of

London at the time it was many days before anyone found her. By the time they did her body had been partially consumed by rats.

Magnus told me that his life review left him feeling devastated. It was the first time in his existence that he'd felt some shame and remorse.

As a result of his review Magnus was told that he had to explore the afterlife and find the girl. This didn't take him long, he told me.

Soon afterwards he found this girl walking towards him. It was a difficult moment for him, he admitted. The girl had every right to condemn him. Indeed he fully expected her to lay into him. She was fully entitled to call him every name under the sun.

And yet she didn't. Instead she forgave him.

SPIRIT SECRET
You can't avoid the past, no one can do that. But if you are part of events that you regret then you have to move on from them. You have to make amends if you can, and then leave the past behind. You have to evolve from there. That's what progression is all about.

After his meeting with the housemaid, Magnus decided that he would dedicate the rest of his existence to being of service.

He confessed to me that, at first, he didn't know what that would mean. He told me that he hadn't considered being a guide because he had no understanding of it. But with the help of the powers-that-be he became one. Apparently he was allocated to me as a guide when I was born, being given the role by what he calls The Enlightened Ones.

The relationship that we have has evolved over the years. During the early part of my life I was just aware that he was there. I think that during that time he was a watcher. But then, when I became a trance medium in particular, I reached a point in my life where I needed the help of a guide on a regular basis. Magnus filled that role.

Back in the early 1990s Two Worlds Publishing produced a book called *Inspired of Spirit* which included some of Magnus's trance teachings. It sold all over the world.

He has been my guide now for more than a quarter of a century. As with any companion, whether in this life or the next, he is not a perfect being. He is a highly articulate and intelligent man but he is also short-tempered. He can be very abrupt and blunt at times, but he's also unbelievably compassionate. He doesn't want to talk too much about his earthly life. I know he was born in 1820 and he passed over in 1903 at the age of 83. But that's about all I do know.

He has told me he is part of a collective of souls called 'The Diamond', so-called because, like a diamond, they are multi-faceted. He says his existence now is about making amends for what he did on this earthly plane. By doing so he has found himself a sort of peace.

His is a lesson we would all do well to heed. Forgiveness can come to us all.

We are not human beings having a spiritual experience. We are spiritual beings having a human experience. TEILHARD DE CHARDIN

Sorry, Son

One of the most memorable messages I have passed on during my career came through at the Hammersmith Apollo during the first of the hugely successful 'Three Mediums' shows.

The shows, in which I appeared with two other leading mediums, Derek Acorah and Tony Stockwell, were a phenomenal hit. Three and a half thousand people turned up and there was an incredibly charged atmosphere.

Inevitably, in an audience of that size, there was a huge mixture of people gathered there. Many were regular visitors to my demonstrations. There was also a mix of the curious, the open-minded and the downright doubtful.

One of the sceptics was a young man called Christian. He was one of the poor unfortunates I often refer to in my warm-up before a demonstration: the ones that have been dragged along.

Initially the message seemed to be intended for his girlfriend. I felt myself in the presence of a young man who had forced his way on to the stage with a wheelchair. He also mentioned the name Christian but it was the details of his illness that seemed to connect to his girlfriend.

'My cousin died of spina bifida,' she said.

Christian had stood up briefly but sat down immediately she confirmed this. He clearly didn't want the spotlight on him. He didn't remain in the dark for long.

It was soon clear to me that the man in the wheelchair wanted to speak to Christian. He had been watching him, it was obvious.

'He says he was with you when you made a crack the other day about how "all someone's car needed was fluffy dice".'

'That's my boss's car,' Christian laughed.

The spirit then began showing me Christian running across a rooftop. He recognised this immediately.

'You're afraid of firearms,' I then went on to say.

'Yes, I'm a medic in the Army,' he smiled.

It was then that the message took an unexpected turn. Suddenly I was aware of another, very anxious male presence entering my consciousness.

At first I thought I heard the name Sorenson. For a second or two I was thinking of Swedish connections. Sorenson is a common Scandinavian name. But then I realised that what he was actually saying was 'sorry, son'. I immediately relayed this to Christian.

'I have a gentleman here; he is speaking very fast and there is a real sense of urgency about him. He is saying "sorry, son".'

This didn't seem to need any explanation for Christian. Suddenly, out of nowhere, this big, tough-looking soldier started looking very tearful.

The man's voice picked up in intensity. 'I am sorry, son, that I didn't understand and I'm sorry that I wasn't there for your proudest moment,' I said.

He nodded at this.

'But I was there, I was watching you.'

Christian was now very emotional indeed.

The man then gave me a rather funny image. 'He is showing me you standing at some kind of passing-out parade wearing a cap that doesn't fit very well. It was a bit on the big side and he says you ended up looking like a mushroom,' I said.

Christian was, by now, crying openly. But he was also laughing at the same time. 'I'm believing it now, you're right,' he said.

I felt the spirit's huge relief at having made contact and he began to fade. Before he went, however, he shared one last thought. 'He says: "Despite the fact I said what I said, you have never dishonoured me."'

The reading brought the house down and everyone applauded Christian, including me.

The camera crew filming the event managed to talk to him afterwards. He said that he had been overwhelmed by the message. It turned out that the anxious man who came through at the end of the message was an uncle who had recently passed away and with whom Christian had had a very difficult but close relationship.

He had also been a soldier and they had fallen out in advance of Christian's passing out. Before the uncle could make amends he had passed over to the other side. Christian had been ready to forgive him, but death had come between them.

The uncle had clearly felt the same way. He had obviously said something he had deeply regretted, and had been desperate to reconnect with his nephew to set the record straight.

I felt proud to have been able to pass it on and to provide an opportunity for the two of them to make their peace on either side of life.

Brotherly Love

I've often talked about how close a connection I had to my maternal grandfather, Laurie. He was the first spirit I encountered when I was a young boy. He came to say goodbye to me the night he died and remained a constant guiding force in my life for many years. Even now, more than thirty years later, I still feel his calming presence around me every now and again.

I didn't only connect with him directly, however. On one memorable occasion I also got a message from him via another medium, Robin Stevens.

Robin was a really gifted medium and a lovely man who has, sadly, passed over himself now. He died far too young and was a great loss to the world of mediumship.

He gave me a message at a spiritualist rally in Hove in the late 1980s. His description of a small, slightly stooped figure, with darkness around one of his eyes, was instantly recognisable as my granddad Laurie.

He had spoken to Robin about something that he'd never communicated to me: his relationship with his brother George.

My granddad Laurie was not a strong man in his youth; he had quite a small build and a weak eye. He also had a deformity in his back; he was a hunchback. Families can be cruel and Laurie had an older brother George who used to play on his young sibling's frailty, teasing and bullying him constantly.

My grandfather wasn't a man to whine or grumble. He was a very positive person who always lived in the present. He was also the kindest, sweetest man in the world; he wouldn't have hurt a fly. So while he'd never mentioned to me about the way he suffered in his youth he had confided in my grandmother and it was she who told me about it.

'How did granddad end up being blind in one eye?' I asked her one day, rather innocently.

She explained that one of the things his brother used to do was make Laurie go cross-eyed. This didn't help his eyesight at all and almost certainly contributed to the fact that by his late twenties my granddad was blind in one eye. For the rest of his life he had to wear glasses with a frosted lens so that the blind eye didn't show.

George and Laurie had never really made their peace on this side of life. George had passed over many years before Laurie so, it seemed, the opportunity for some kind of reconciliation had been lost for ever.

Robin Stevens had never heard me speak about my grandfather and knew nothing about my relationship with him. He described what had happened when Laurie had come through to him.

'Laurie says that now he has a straight back and both his eyes are clear and blue,' Robin said.

That made me smile immediately. I remembered how granddad's one good eye was incredibly clear and blue.

Robin also described accurately how Laurie had this huge lipoma, a big fatty lump on his arm. Physically he was quite a deformed man, but his kindness shone through.

The most important piece of information Robin had for me, however, was that Laurie wanted me to know that he'd finally forgiven his brother for all the horrible things he'd done to him during his life. They had been reunited on the other side and the troubles they'd had together on this earthly plane had been overcome.

The timing of the message was quite significant.

The last of Laurie's surviving siblings, his elder sister—and my great-aunt—Dolly had just passed over. He told Robin that he'd met her on the other side already.

I found his message very moving. It also made me think more deeply about the afterlife.

It made me realise, for instance, that sometimes the person who can help you the most is the person that you ridicule or revile the most. A lot of people assume that the spirits best placed to help them here on earth are their nearest and dearest. The last people they expect to be of comfort to them are those with whom they didn't get on in life. But that's not necessarily the case, as George and Laurie may have found out.

Mostly, however, the message made me think about forgiveness. Forgiveness can be a difficult thing to achieve and sometimes it is beyond us, on this side of life. When I thought of all the awful things George had done to my granddad when they were boys I could understand why. It must have affected Laurie deeply and left him with emotional wounds he carried all his life.

In this life he hadn't been ready—or able—to forgive. But that had changed on the other side. Eternity had proven too long a time to bear a grudge.

Both parties have to be ready. The person that needs to be forgiven needs to be able to feel remorse and want genuinely to be forgiven. And I think the person who is doing the forgiving needs to have put the pain to bed. George and Laurie hadn't reached that point—in this life. But after hearing from Laurie, I knew that they had on the other side.

I found that very reassuring. And I think we can all draw comfort from it.

The Glass Butterfly

One question that crops up time and again when I'm talking to people is this: can I communicate with people who speak in languages other than my native tongue, English?

It's understandable why people might think this could be a problem, but in reality it isn't one at all.

That's because spirits don't communicate through me in a conventional or normal language. The connection I make with them operates on a level of vibration. This means that they can transmit thoughts, images, smells, sounds and feelings into my conscious mind.

As a result of this I am able to communicate in foreign languages. A spirit may be speaking in a foreign tongue but to me it comes through as a vibration that I am able to easily interpret. As long as I can see the images, hear the sounds and smell the smells they are communicating to me, it doesn't matter whether they are talking English, Russian or Mandarin.

Now, as always in my work, there are exceptions to the rule. Sometimes, for instance, I will be given words in the spirit's native tongue for a very particular purpose. Normally it is for evidential reasons, to help the recipient of the message recognise the person who is trying to communicate with them. What happens in this instance is that I attempt to speak the words phonetically as they have been spoken to me. It can often produce quite dramatic results.

The most striking example of this occurred when, in 1999, the Japanese Spiritualist Society invited me to help celebrate the fiftieth anniversary of spiritualism in Japan.

The Japanese are fascinated by the Western style of mediumship because it is very different from the Japanese style. A lot of it over there is tied in with Shinto religion, which means that it is extremely respectful and formal. It is very much based on ritual and is conducted in a highly reverent way with the mediums mostly in trance.

A congregation or a gathering never speaks directly to the medium or the communicating spirit. It is all done through a chairman, or a master, and the master is the only person who speaks directly to the spirits through the medium. Everyone else must direct their comments or pleas to their loved ones, or ancestors as they like to call them, through the master of the ceremony. I find it quite fascinating.

Mediumship around the world is evolving all the time, however. There are one or two mavericks over there who have, a bit like me, taken the art out of the religious environment and into the theatres and on to television, but they are very rare. And the Japanese are absolutely fascinated by the very informal, almost conversational style in which we European and Western mediums work.

The trip was a huge honour for me at the time. While I was there I was asked to lecture, do some séances, and do a demonstration. It was a curious experience for me, as I'm sure it was for the audience. Japanese people don't applaud—they bow—so it was very strange to have all these people dipping their heads to me as I entered the room for the demonstration.

I was working with a translator over there. As I was giving the reading she was at the front doing the translation. I was quite fortunate because she'd spent quite a lot of time in the West. So she was fairly animated in her language, which worked well for me during the demonstrations.

Although, as I always explain, communications come through to me on the vibration of thought, sometimes spirits will put things through in an indigenous language if it is important for evidential reasons. This is what happened during one message.

During the course of this reading I felt myself in the presence of a man. He was elderly, quite a grand, almost aristocratic-looking gentleman. He was directing me quite clearly to a lady who was sitting in the front row. Through the interpreter I quickly identified her as his daughter. She seemed a little apprehensive at this.

All of a sudden my mind was filled with this Japanese word which I said phonetically. As I say, Japanese people don't show emotion in public. They are very self-controlled: it's part of their culture. In particular it's not expected for women to show emotion; they are almost expected to behave as if they are subservient. I found this quite difficult at first but I grew to accept it as time went on. I realised it was part of their culture and that it wasn't my place to try to change it.

Knowing how emotionless Japanese women were reputed to be, it made the lady's reaction when I said this word all the more shocking. The instant I said it she became very emotional. She was crying and smiling at the same time.

'Why does this mean so much?' the translator asked the lady.

'The word that Mr Fry just used was an affectionate name that only my father ever called me,' she said. 'It means glass butterfly.'

As the message went on, it was clear that the father had a powerful reason for contacting his daughter. It was also clear that the message was actually quite controversial.

It transpired that this woman was a fairly mature woman and she had in the past year or so divorced her husband. We didn't go into the circumstances but it was clear that it was a cruel and unhappy marriage which she had endured for a number of years.

As I connected with her father, I sensed that he had brokered the marriage when he was alive and was very traditional in his views and outlook on life. To avoid upsetting him his daughter had suffered in silence while he was alive. Soon after he had passed over, however, she had sought a divorce.

Now, of course in Japanese society divorce was considered a no-no. This was quite clear from the reaction of the audience as I continued the communication. I remember them sitting there very, very quietly, not quite approving of what was going on. One or two were murmuring to themselves as if to say: 'Who is this woman who brought shame on her family?'

The lady admitted that, ever since his passing, she had worried that her father, whom she had adored, was ashamed or disapproved of her. She believed that he thought she had dishonoured the family by taking this very unusual step after he died.

But as I channelled his thoughts I gave her reassurance that this was not the case.

'I know why you did what you did,' he said through me. 'And I understand what you did. You had no alternative. Your husband was dishonouring you. By leaving him you didn't dishonour me, you honoured me.'

By the end of the message the lady was in even more of an emotional state. Many in the audience were dabbing their cheeks with handkerchiefs too.

I felt immensely proud to have put the issue to rest for them both.

The Two Wolves

One of the most profound pieces of wisdom I read as a young man was an old Cherokee Indian story. It was passed on anonymously so I don't know who first told it. But I do know it holds a message that we would all do well to carry with us.

According to the story an elderly Cherokee wise man was talking to his grandson. 'We all have a great battle going on inside us,' he told the boy. 'It is a terrible fight and it is between two wolves.

'One wolf is evil. Inside him lives anger, envy, sorrow, regret, greed, arrogance, self-pity, guilt, resentment, inferiority, lies, false pride, superiority, self-doubt and ego. The other wolf is good. Inside him lives joy, peace, love, hope, serenity, humility, kindness, benevolence, empathy, generosity, truth, compassion and faith.'

The elder went on and told the boy that this fight was going on inside him right now. And it would continue all his life. The little boy sat thoughtfully for a moment then turned to ask his grandfather a question.

'Which wolf will win?' he said.

The Cherokee chief smiled at him and said simply: 'The one you feed.'

HOW THE SPIRITS REWARD YOUR PATIENCE

The Power of Perseverance

The spirit world can guide us all through the difficult periods in our life. If we tune in and listen carefully to what it is telling us, we can benefit from the accumulated wisdom it has to offer.

This is something I know from personal experience. The spirit dimension has offered me some valuable personal advice during the course of my life, but perhaps the most important thing it has taught me is patience.

There was a time when I didn't possess it at all. Like most teenagers and young men I was impatient to get on with my life. I wanted everything and I wanted it now. Or sooner.

This was particularly true when I began to see that I had a gift and that I was meant to do something with it.

By the time I was in my late twenties I was building a reputation as a medium. I was also doing well professionally in my retail job. I was making good money and, in general, I was happy with my life.

But, as I've mentioned earlier, I always had this feeling that I was meant to be doing more. That I was meant to be moving along more quickly, that things needed to happen faster for me.

By this time I had a good relationship with the

spirit world.

I had learned a great deal from it. So I turned to it for help and guidance regularly. During this period I turned to it frequently to ask the same question: 'What should I be doing next?'

The answer was always the same: 'Wait.'

At the time I wasn't very happy about this. I was an impatient child. 'Wait' wasn't a good enough answer. Now I know why. Looking back I can see that I had to have more life experience, more life, more joy, more pain. I needed it so that I could channel it into my mediumship, so that I could interpret the knowledge the spirit world was passing on to me and pass it on to those who really needed wisdom and guidance.

That's what the spirit world has shown me over the years. Experience life first, because that is how you will learn, how you will become more wise. Seek instant rewards in life and you will never find them.

Maybe one day I will write my autobiography and tell the full story of how much joy and pain, and hurt, I have experienced in life—but not yet.

The Empty Seat

The spirit world is very determined. If at first it doesn't succeed, it will try and try—and try—again. Experience has taught me this, so there are times when, during demonstrations or readings, I have to be extremely persistent too.

The most memorable example happened when I was in Oxford doing a demonstration at a theatre a few years ago. Early on I felt myself in the presence of a young man. It was a very clear and precise connection and the information he was giving me was very specific. He was guiding me towards the top row of the theatre in search of a particular person.

'I have a man here who is telling me his name is Stephen McCready and he is looking to speak to a Doreen. He wants to talk about his wife Kate and his daughter Sharon,' I said.

By any standards this was a very detailed piece of information so I was very surprised when this drew no reaction among the audience.

The spirit wasn't deterred; in fact he gave me even more specific information. Suddenly my mind was filled with images of smoke and flames billowing out of an upper-storey window. I felt a pain in my lungs.

'This man is showing me that he was killed in a house fire,' I said.

Again he was steering me towards the upper reaches of the auditorium. In fact this time he was even pointing at a particular seat.

I knew he was right, I could feel that the energy he was seeking was there. One of the runners who pass the microphone around the audience went tearing up the steps to the precise seat but found it was empty.

I was confused. 'The connection is there, in that seat,' I said. 'I'm going to keep going back until I sort this out.'

I must have let my frustration show a little because one or two members of the audience started to titter. The days when something like this threw me were long gone, of course. 'I don't care if some of you think it's funny, that's where I want to be,' I said.

Reluctantly, however, I accepted that, for now, I had to move away and give another message. But as I moved on the spirit of the young man didn't go away.

During the interval my agent at the time came up to me and suggested that I forget about pursuing the message in the second half. 'Drop it, Colin—drop it, please,' she said.

'No, I can't drop it,' I said, a bit miffed. 'I know what I am getting.'

'Well, the audience is starting to look uncomfortable and you're going to make yourself look stupid,' she warned.

By now I was getting a tad angry. 'Look, I know there is a message that I have to get across to the person in that seat. And I'm going to carry on until I get that message to the person in that seat. OK?'

I was actually getting quite annoyed with myself too. I didn't doubt myself. I knew that this lad kept taking me up to that corner and he wouldn't be doing that if there wasn't a reason. Was I missing something? Was I getting a piece of information wrong? It started to play on my mind a little.

I began the second half of the show with some other messages, but all the time I felt the presence of the young man from earlier. He was lingering, waiting to get his message across. He wasn't going away.

So towards the end of the show I returned to him. 'I'm sorry, ladies and gentlemen, but the young man I connected with earlier is insisting I go back up there to the top of the theatre,' I said. I saw one or two people in the audience shifting uneasily in their seats. I think some people were feeling embarrassed on my behalf.

I sent the runner up again. Again there was no response.

I was really angry with myself now. I couldn't believe I was going to let this man down and not connect with someone on his behalf. Reluctantly, however, I made the decision to drop it.

The rest of the show went well enough although I knew, deep down, that I wasn't firing in all cylinders because of the frustration I was feeling.

But then, just as I was approaching the moment where I was going to wind down the demonstration, I noticed something out of the corner of my eye. High up in the theatre, where I'd kept sending the runner, there was movement.

I looked up into the half-lit area of the auditorium and saw a guy emerging through a side door and slipping into the seat that we'd found empty throughout the evening.

As soon as I finished the message I was involved in, I headed straight back up there.

There were one or two groans when I said I was going back up there again. They soon dissipated when they realised there was now someone sitting in the seat.

When the runner arrived at the man's side I began to go through the information again.

'I have a young man called Stephen McCready who wants to connect with Doreen. He has shown me that he died in a house fire. He also wants to speak about his wife Kate and his daughter Sharon.'

The man looked a little taken aback, to say the least. He took the microphone, and in a strong Irish accent, said, 'My name's not Doreen, it's Dorian.'

This got a huge laugh, of course, but I didn't have time to join in the fun. 'Dorian, this is very serious,' I said. 'Do you understand the name Stephen McCready and a fire?'

'Yes,' he replied.

The house was silent now. No one was giggling.

He continued, 'I was the fireman who pulled Steve McCready out of the fire in which he died. He was also a friend of mine. I know his wife, Kate, and his daughter, Sharon.'

Half the audience started applauding, the other half sat there in complete shock. One or two of those who had been giggling simply sat there shaking their heads in disbelief.

I wasn't interested in proving a point, however. My job was to deliver an important message. 'Stephen is showing me that his wife and daughter are now living in Dublin,' I said to Dorian.

'Yes, that's correct,' he confirmed.

'He's also showing me that you will be seeing them in the near future.'

'Yes, we're going over there next month,' he nodded.

'I have a very important message from Stephen for you, Dorian. The message is this . . . if that man who is living with his wife ever touches his daughter again he will come back and he will haunt him for the rest of his life.'

The theatre was completely silent by now. Dorian, however, seemed to understand what I was saying.

'I know exactly what that's about, Colin,' he said.

'You do?'

'Yes, I do. Leave it to me. I will sort it out.'

44

I can't remember a more spontaneous eruption of applause. The audience were soon filing out of the theatre, almost every one of them talking about 'the fireman's message'.

After the show I spoke briefly to Dorian. He was a lovely, down-to-earth guy.

'I didn't want to be here,' he said. 'It's my wife that wanted to come. I'd gone out to the bar for most of the show. I only came in with five minutes to go to pick my wife up.'

I was intrigued to know why none of what I was saying meant anything to his wife.

'She didn't know anything about this Steve McCready and I guess she didn't equate Doreen with Dorian,' he said.

He admitted that his opinion of me in particular and mediums in general had been altered for ever by what had happened tonight. 'I'm stunned, to be honest,' he confessed. 'There's no way you could possibly have known any of that.'

For me in all of the years that I've been doing what I do, it has remained one of my most memorable messages. It's memorable not because it looked like I was getting it wrong, nor that I was vindicated in such dramatic fashion within the last minutes of the demonstration. To me it's memorable because it illustrated so powerfully how determined spirits can be to pass on messages, especially important ones like the one Stephen passed on to his friend Dorian.

Damson Jam

One summer's day, I was sitting in my conservatory looking at the damsons that were growing in my garden.

'Come on, hurry up, I want you to ripen so that I can make some jam,' I started thinking to myself.

No sooner had I done so than I heard the voice of my guide Magnus in my ear. 'Just let nature do what it's supposed to do,' he said. 'They will be ready when they are ready. In the meantime you should go and do something else.'

In life you can't sit around and wait for something rewarding to happen, because if you do—it won't happen.

Something else is taking care of the rewards that come to you in life. While they do so you have to go out and live your life.

'Psychism, Spiritualism, Mediumship is not necessarily something one should assume should happen when you think it should happen.' LESLIE FLINT

Waiting In The Wings

Many people in the spiritualist movement think the world of mediumship should be a private members club, closed off to the outside world. So it's not surprising that these people disapprove of mediums like me performing in public places such as theatres.

I think they are totally wrong for all sorts of reasons.

To begin with theatres are very energetic and highly charged places. They have seen all of life's dramas played out on their stages. People have laughed and cried and been moved in all sorts of ways while sitting there. I think it's a great environment for a medium to work. Apart from anything else it often provides a little bit of drama in its own right.

I remember one night in Bournemouth many years ago when I was connecting with a young girl who had passed over. The message she was passing on to me was very clear and strong: she wanted to connect with a friend of hers. Try as I might, however, I couldn't locate this friend in the audience. I felt she was near one of the exits so kept saying, 'She's over here by the door.'

It was very frustrating, especially because I felt the spirit was exuding such energy. This lady really was determined to make a connection.

I was just about to give up and move on when I noticed an usherette standing in a doorway at the side of the audience.

I immediately sensed some energy around her and asked her to step out into the main area of the theatre.

She was reluctant at first. 'I'm not sure if I'm allowed to do this, but I think it's for me,' she said, looking nervously around for the theatre manager. Fortunately a member of the management was around and he nodded his permission for her to accept the message.

I was staging this particular performance in the town's new conference centre but this lady had also been an usherette at the old theatre in the town, The Winter Gardens, which had been knocked down.

The spirit with whom I was connecting had also been an usherette at the old theatre. I got the feeling that the two friends had been like sisters, inseparable.

The message was a very simple and heartfelt

one. The lady had come through to thank the usherette for all the help she'd provided when she'd been dying of cancer.

It was a very touching message, one that moved many in the audience to tears, although I'm sure there were one or two sceptics who thought it was all fixed. It wasn't. It was simply more evidence of just how tenacious and determined the spirit world can be when it needs to connect with someone.

A Birthday Greeting

One of the challenging things about working in a large auditorium with thousands of people sitting in front of me is finding the person who is meant to receive a particular communication.

So many members of the audience are keen to get a message that they often interpret the details they are hearing as applying to them and raise their arm for the microphone without really thinking. As a result, I often have to be quite sceptical about those who stand up and start waving at me almost the instant I offer the first piece of evidence.

It's happened countless times: I will offer up a name, let's say, Violet. Before I can say anything else someone is grabbing the microphone and telling me, 'That's for me, I had a second cousin twice removed whose middle name was Violet.'

I don't blame them for being enthusiastic and eager to receive a communication. I do understand the need of so many who come to hear from a loved one. But I do wish sometimes that they were a little more patient in listening to the evidence.

This is why I am always pleased when a spirit

begins their communication by showing me something very specific that can only apply to one person in the audience.

So it was on this particular evening, when I sensed myself in the presence of the spirit of a very strong lady. It was as if she knew that time was limited and she needed to get through to her loved one as fast as possible because she began showing me a very clear image.

'I am being shown a letter or a card that this lady wrote to her daughter. It's been folded twice, so that it's now creased into four sections,' I said. 'The letter or card is with the lady here in the theatre tonight.'

As if this wasn't enough, the lady passed on even more information. 'I'm also being shown that the person who is carrying this letter has come to see me before in the hope of getting a message,' I said.

I wasn't surprised when I saw some activity high up in the upper circle of the theatre. I quickly spotted a lady dipping into her handbag and then getting to her feet.

'Do you recognise what this lady is saying?' I asked her.

'Yes, I do,' she said, holding out a piece of paper.

It was clearly a treasured memento because it was sheathed in plastic, for protection.

'This is the last letter I got from my mother.'

'Do you understand what I am saying about you having been to see me before?'

'Yes,' she said. 'This is the second time I've come to one of your demonstrations.'

I could feel that it was an emotional moment for the lady.

'It's my birthday,' she told me, dabbing away at her tears with a handkerchief. 'I came along tonight in the hope that my mother might try to get through to me on my birthday.'

'OK, my love,' I said. 'Well, you've got your wish and she's definitely here.'

Her mother's message was a rather beautiful one.

'She is asking me to tell you that she still believes every word she put in that letter,' I said. 'And she wants you to know that there isn't a day goes by when she doesn't come to see you.'

She also told her daughter that she had to accept that she'd been content to leave this life when she did, even though it meant causing such grief.

'I passed from this life at exactly the right time because if I had carried on I would not have been happy, I would not have been one hundred per cent me,' she said.

Her daughter nodded at this.

As the reading went on it was clear the lady had a cheeky sense of humour. It was also clear that she had been a difficult person to please during her life here.

'I don't like my favourite place any more,' she told me.

At first her daughter looked perplexed. She didn't know what her mother meant. Soon, however, she realised her mother was talking about the large garden they had at the rear of their home.

In the past year or so a new neighbour had moved in and cut down some huge Leylandii that separated the two properties.

'She used to hate those Leylandii,' her daughter said. 'I'd have thought she would like the garden now.'

'No, she doesn't like the fact that it's lost its privacy,' I said. Her daughter just chuckled as if to say 'typical'.

The lady had another gripe she wanted to pass on too. 'Did you spray perfume on her when she was laid out after her death?' I asked her daughter.

She nodded.

'It was very sweet of you, dear, but it was the wrong perfume. It smelled like fly spray.'

When the daughter protested that it was a bottle she'd found in her mother's things, she quipped, 'And it was full, why do you think it was full?'

The message illustrated something that I've come to realise more and more over the years. There is no doubt in my mind that objects or mementoes help draw spirits towards their loved ones. It is as if it is a beacon, a light to which they are attracted. It is why I encourage all those who come to one of my demonstrations to bring with them something that is going to be significant and meaningful to the spirit of their loved one.

In this case it was that oh-so-precious letter that the mother had written to her daughter during her final days on this plane. It proved a beacon that guided her spirit to come through and deliver a very special birthday message.

The other, deeper truth it underlined was something that I've grown to understand more and more over the years. Persistence is important if you are to receive a message from the other side. You cannot just turn up at a spiritualist church or go along to a medium privately and expect to get the connection you want just like that, at the click of your fingers. It simply doesn't work that way.

You have to dedicate yourself to it. You have to be serious about it. I once encountered a lady who had been to see me more than two dozen times before she got a message.

After receiving it, however, she said she would have carried on coming even if she'd been to two thousand shows.

The lady who had come along on her birthday had demonstrated the same level of commitment. And the spirit world had rewarded her for it.

SPIRIT SECRET
It doesn't matter what decade you are in, the experiences of joy and pain have the potential to help you grow.

You can't sit back when things aren't going right. You need to process and understand what has happened to you and then maybe you can make sure it doesn't happen again.

Geraldine's Journey

'Our birth is but a sleep and a forgetting;
The Soul that rises with us, our life's Star,
Hath had elsewhere its setting. And cometh
from afar.'
WILLIAM WORDSWORTH

Spirits can reveal themselves much, much sooner than this, of course. I have often been contacted by spirits within hours of their passing.

The most remarkable message in this respect

was the one I got from Geraldine, the lady who had been so instrumental in leading me into the world of mediumship.

Together with various other circle members, Geraldine, John and I sat in a circle for fourteen years. Every now and again one of us might be away or ill but in the main we met every week.

Geraldine's health had been fading over the years and eventually she fell very ill. We knew it was only a matter of time.

I will never forget the day she passed over. I had travelled with another member of the circle, a lady called Pat, to Norwich for the day. We were standing in Norwich Cathedral when we both felt something. We just turned and looked at each other. Instinctively we both knew what we'd just felt. Geraldine had left this earthly plane and passed over to the other side.

We phoned John immediately and he said, 'Yes, she's just gone.'

She passed away on a Friday and her funeral was on the following Monday. There was no service as such. John, his son and his grandchildren went into the crematorium where they had a bit of nice music and watched the coffin go through the curtain.

As I've mentioned, there had been a time after their son died when they'd lost their faith. But since they'd made contact with him and had formed a regular circle, their belief in the afterlife had become unshakeable.

'We didn't need it, life goes on,' John said. 'It's not what Geraldine and I believe.'

We sat in a circle on the following Tuesday night. Geraldine had been gone for four days and she came through and spoke to us in her own voice.

It was as if she hadn't left the room, let alone left this life. Her spirit was as close to us as it had ever been.

Heinz Baked Beans

Understanding exactly what I am being shown by a spirit can be a challenge sometimes. I am shown images, feel sensations, smell aromas, hear sounds. I can sometimes feel as if I am being overloaded by sensory experiences.

It can be very challenging, but again the key is to be patient and to remember that the spirit with whom I am communicating has made a huge effort to get through to me. The least I can do in return is to persevere.

I remember once a lady came to see me. She was a lovely lady, a schoolteacher, and she'd travelled all the way from the Isle of Wight.

Her husband came through in the reading and as he did so he began showing me all sorts of nautical things—ship's wheels, ropes tied in specialist sailing knots, canvas sails.

'Do you understand that?' I asked.

'Oh yes, very much,' the lady smiled. 'That sounds right.'

She was a very proper and disciplined lady, I could tell. She had clearly read up on how to behave—and not behave—in a reading with a medium, and let me do all the talking, merely confirming things with a nodded yes or a shake of the head for no.

To be honest, there were very few nos.

The moment she was absolutely sure it was her husband was when I began describing something else I was being shown. 'My darling, I'm being shown a tin of Heinz baked beans,' I said, slightly hesitantly. 'Do you like Heinz baked beans?' I wondered.

'No, but I know what he means,' she said, smiling.

I didn't understand it at all. But I was happy that she had understood it, and I continued with the reading.

It was a lovely, warm connection. It wasn't particularly dramatic, but it gave her all the reassurance she needed that he had passed over to a safe place.

After I'd brought the reading to a close, I couldn't help but ask her to explain what some of the details meant.

'Well, the sailing references were from his time in the Merchant Navy,' she said. 'He was also a keen yachtsman throughout his life.'

'And what about the Heinz baked beans?' I asked. 'That was the one thing that left me stumped.'

I was expecting some complex explanation but, as so often in life, the answer was much simpler.

'Oh, he was German and that was his name,' she said. 'His name was Heinz!'

I couldn't stop myself from bursting into a fit of the giggles. It was, in many ways, the most obvious sign I could possibly have been given. I just hadn't picked up on it.

A Word Out Of Place

The spirit world can move in mysterious ways. So I don't always understand what I'm being shown and the implications of what I'm being shown. Sometimes this lack of clarity is down to the quality of thought that is being channelled through me. Sometimes an energy can be weak, at other times it can be too confused. But there are times when the only reason I can't properly interpret a message is that I have been using a single wrong word.

During the early days of filming my television series *6ixth Sense*, for instance, I was directed by the spirit I was connected with to a woman who was sitting in the audience.

'My dear, I have your father with me and your father is telling me that he wants to congratulate you about your fantasy about the opera singer,' I said.

She just looked at me blankly and shook her head. 'No, I'm sorry, Colin—it doesn't make sense at all.'

But he wouldn't let me move away from her.

'I'm so sorry,' I said. 'He's insisting that you have been living with this fantasy in your head for months.'

Again she looked nonplussed.

I persevered for another few minutes and was about to give up when her father gave me an image of her sitting at a typewriter or a keyboard, writing.

'Would you understand that?' I asked.

'Oh yes, I'm an author and I have just finished writing a novel,' she said.

'A novel. Is it about opera or an opera singer?'

'Yes, it is,' she said. 'The heroine is an opera

56

singer.'

I could have sworn, I was so frustrated—with myself more than anything else. 'Why did I see the word "fantasy" and not the word "novel"?' I asked myself. 'I'd have saved myself a lot of time, effort and frustration.'

A Determined Soul

I have performed demonstrations in all sorts of venues, all over the world, from the most historic theatres to the most modern conference centres. It's an interesting fact that it is often the older buildings that produce the most responsive and welcoming atmosphere for spirit communication. It's almost as if the theatres with more character encourage spirits with more character to emerge.

A show I did at the lovely old Theatre Royal in Brighton illustrates the point.

I like to think of it as my local theatre. I've performed there many times over the years and always attract a large and enthusiastic crowd. This particular night was no exception. It was packed with a mixture of people young and old, male and female, straight and gay. It was Brighton, after all.

People often ask me how it is that some spirits are able to communicate with their loved ones on a regular basis, while others never, ever come through.

It's a difficult question to answer because, truth be told, it's unclear. I don't claim to understand the afterlife in all its infinite complexity. During more than thirty years working as a medium, I have been given some insights into the other side. But until I go there myself, I too won't know exactly how existence operates there.

One of the things I do know about the spirit world, however, is that there are those spirits who make an enormous effort to communicate with this earthly plane.

Often it is because they have important information to share. So it proved with the young man who came through at the Theatre Royal that night.

I had a strong sense of the boy's personality from the moment he began trying to communicate with me. He was a livewire now, as he was in life. I suspected he was a lad who had lived on the edge. I also sensed he might have died in controversial circumstances.

'He's showing me that he is very angry that his favourite club has been closed down,' I said. 'He's also showing me how he used to go there when he was under age.'

At first no one in the theatre recognised him. This only served to strengthen his resolve, however, and he was soon directing me towards the back of the large audience and a middle-aged woman who was sitting on her own.

She was unconvinced that it was him at first. 'That doesn't sound like my son,' she said.

He soon persuaded her, however.

'He is showing me that you asked for him to come through tonight,' I said. 'He is showing you asking three times today, at 10.30 am, 2.30 pm and again at around 6.30 pm, half an hour before coming to the theatre,' I said.

She was stunned at this. 'I'm just surprised he's come through to me again. He has communicated with me before,' she said.

The boy admitted that it had been hard for him to get through.

'I had to argue my case, but I promised my mum that I would come through,' he told me.

It wasn't just to answer his mother's request that he had come through, however.

I had to encourage him to make one final push to finish his message. 'He's using a very bad word that I can't repeat here,' I said. 'And he is using it to describe the people who gave evidence at the inquest.'

He also used some words to describe the magistrate. 'He was deaf, blind and stupid,' I said, censoring his words a little.

The reason he had come through tonight was to thank his mother and someone else for speaking up for him in the courtroom. He was also angry at the injustice that surrounded his death.

'Because of your efforts my name has been exonerated,' he said.

She understood this and nodded.

He continued, 'I want to thank you and Andy for doing that.'

By now the connection with him was growing weaker by the second. I sent out a thought to him, asking him to pass on a message of love to his mother. I sensed that in life, perhaps, he didn't do that as often as he might have.

'My mum don't need me to tell her I love her,' he told me. I passed this on to her.

She smiled sadly. 'No, you don't, son. I love you too—and I miss you very much.'

It was a very emotional message and brought a tear to the eye of most of the people in the auditorium that night.

It illustrated something that I've grown to understand about the afterlife: that often there are messages that simply have to get through, no matter what the obstacles.

SPIRIT SECRET
There are ways in which you can make yourself available for a message. If you are hoping that a loved one is going to communicate with you, you have to do a few things. First of all you have to put yourself into situations where they are going to communicate. The most obvious ways of doing this are by attending spiritualist churches or visiting psychic centres, going along to talks about the subject of spirit communication or reading some books on the subject.

It's also very important to talk to the spirit world. You need to develop an attitude where you accept that while you cannot hear, feel or see them, they can hear, feel and see you. That means that if you want them to communicate with you, you have to communicate with them.

Next time you go shopping, if your mum liked going shopping put the thought out that you are going shopping and this one is going to be your day together. If you are missing your daughter or sister, take a moment to say to her, 'I still love you and I still miss you.'

The gap between the spirit world and the earthly plane is always in a state of flux and change. At times they are very close indeed.

By communicating with the spirit world you close that distance even more.

Patient Spirits

I often hear from people who are frustrated that they don't receive messages or communications of any type from their loved ones on the other side. People come up to me at my demonstrations and say things like: 'My son has been passed over for ten years but I've never heard from him.'

It is difficult for these people, I know. There are a number of reasons why they may not have received a connection, one of which is that the spirit in question might be waiting for the right moment.

In many cases spirits can only make a single connection with this earthly plane. So it's logical that in cases like this they are going to wait for the moment when they are going to make the most impact. They are going to wait for the best possible time to come through and make the connection and pass on the information they need to pass on.

A really good example of this happened when I was performing in a charity show in the north of England. Early on in the demonstration I felt a spirit directing me towards the front rows of the theatre.

'I'm feeling I should be down in the fourth row,' I said. 'In fact I am feeling very strongly that I should be with you,' I added as my eyes fell on a particular lady.

I recognised her immediately. She was a middle-aged lady who had been coming to my performances steadily for about four years. She always came to me afterwards and would tell me that she'd been hoping to hear from her mother.

As I do with everyone, I'd told her not to tell me any more than that. 'I don't want to know any more about her.'

Now, at last, she'd got a message.

It was her mother. She was smiling throughout. The elderly man sitting next to her wore a wry smile too.

'You must be the husband. She's directing the energy to you.'

The lady had always come along to my shows on her own. This was, to my knowledge, the first time she'd brought her dad along with her. Maybe that was what her mum had been waiting for. She was biding her time, waiting for the two of them to be together to get her communication across. Maybe it was because she knew she had only the one chance to communicate. It couldn't just be for one—it had to be for the two of them, her husband and her daughter.

4.

HOW THE SPIRITS CAN INSPIRE YOU

'Do not look always to far horizons. You may
be tempted to wish towards them, only to find
another far horizon. And what you have lost
was the joy of the journey and what it can
teach you. Live always in the moment.'
MAGNUS, SPIRIT GUIDE OF COLIN FRY

Every one of us is the sum of all our experiences.
I certainly am.

My childhood wasn't an easy one. I was a very
small child, much smaller than the other kids at
school. I also suffered very badly from asthma. But
I was quite wilful. I was always the kid that asked
why. Why do I need to do this? Why can't I do
that?

My father wanted me to play football and all the
other things that boys were supposed to like. I
remember one Christmas when I was eight or so
I'd opened all my Christmas presents except one.
And when I opened the last parcel I saw a pair of
football boots. And I remember looking at them in
absolute horror, then looking at my dad and
saying: 'Why I have got these? What am I
supposed to do with them?' I will never forget the
look of disappointment on his face.

Later, when I told him that I wanted to do ballet
lessons rather than play football he was horrified. I
never did get to do ballet.

By the time I reached my teenage years I was

the strange child, not just by my family's standards but by everyone's standards. I was much more sensitive than the other children in the family and at school. Often when I tried to express what I was feeling things became very emotional.

To the outside world I was never the tough kid who succeeds. But inside I had this belief that I was going to achieve something in life. It was, of course, being reinforced by the spirits with whom I was already communicating.

What I had to understand was that to live by feeling and emotion was a strength and not a weakness. And as I came to accept that, I also came to realise that I had been born with this gift and I was a strong person. I just had to go through the awful experience of school, of finding that the people who were supposed to be there to protect me were often the bullies; I had to have that experience of being perceived to be weak to find my strength. I still refuse to be a square peg forced into a round hole.

The good news was that once I discovered my strength in this life, I was able to draw on it to acquire even more understanding. This time, from the spirit world.

This is where I am a very fortunate person because I'm not just the sum of my earthly experiences—I am the sum of my spiritual experiences as well.

During the course of my life I've had spiritually quite intimate experiences not just with people who've been close to me but also with total strangers. I always consider it a great honour that someone who has passed over would want to share some intimate part of their life experience with me for the benefit of someone they knew on this side of life. I consider it a particular honour because I've benefited from that, I've gained so much wisdom from that.

Some of the messages I communicate benefit me almost as much as they benefit the recipients. They help me and inspire me in my constant search to learn more about the mysteries of the afterlife.

Speaking In Code

Spirits don't always have a specific purpose for making contact. There are times when they simply want to say 'hello' to someone with whom it might be interesting to have a conversation. In that sense, again, individuals are no different on the other side from how they are on this earthly plane.

I have had some interesting experiences in this respect, and none more interesting than one evening when I was conducting a séance. I was, apparently, channelling Magnus through to the group of people who were in the circle that evening when he made an announcement. 'I am now going to stand to one side for a few moments,' he'd said. 'There is someone here who I would very much like to allow to come through.'

The spirit who Magnus was going to allow to come through wanted to talk to someone in the room who had known him when he was alive. At first he had great difficulty coming through and stammered a lot. Eventually he said his name was Alan and he managed to establish a conversation with a particular lady in the room.

'Can you tell me how we know each other?' the lady asked.

'Oh yes, we used to play together when we were children,' Alan explained. 'And—and your family knew my family.'

In spite of his stammer they talked away quite happily. After a while, however, Alan went on to address a man who was a visitor to our circle. He began by asking the man a question. 'I understand that you work in the field of science,' he said.

'That's correct,' the man said.

'Good,' he replied.

They then started having this very in-depth conversation about computers. And this spirit, Alan, started quoting very complex equations through me.

When it was all over my circle leader asked the lady about it.

'So did you know the man?' he said.

'Oh yes, I knew him well; my parents and his parents were really close friends. He was quite famous in his time. His name was Alan Turing,' she told us.

Well, at this point the scientist visitor almost fell off his chair. 'Alan Turing!' he said. 'Do you have any idea who Alan Turing was?'

I admitted that I didn't.

'Only one of the most brilliant men this country has ever produced! He was probably the father of modern computing,' he said. 'I can't believe I've just had a conversation with Alan Turing.'

The man wasn't a sceptic, far from it, but he was approaching the whole mediumship thing from a scientific point of view. As I mentioned, he was a visitor to the circle and he was investigating what went on in it from a rational standpoint.

So to then get a communication from a man who

was one of the great scientists of his day, talking about his knowledge and about how his work in this world was carrying on in the afterlife, was absolutely amazing to him.

With a look of sheer astonishment on his face, the man turned to me and said, 'Colin, I know there's no way you could have known anything about what he was telling me. You could never have known that stuff we were talking about.

'The stuff we were talking about was really cutting edge technology. We were discussing nanocomputers; the equations he was talking about were very advanced.

'With the greatest respect to you, you're an intelligent man, but they were totally beyond your understanding. I was struggling to keep pace with what the guy was talking about and I'm a scientist.'

The visitor worked in industrial science. He was one of these men who set out on a path of investigation and he'd sat over a number of years with a number of mediums. He had accumulated ongoing evidence. His reward for that open-mindedness was a communication that anyone in his sphere would have died for.

Afterwards I became fascinated by Alan Turing and wanted to find out more about him. I'd never heard of him before.

Some time later there was a play in the West End about his life, *Breaking The Code*. I went to see it and saw what a tragic ending his life had come to. It should never have been that way.

Alan Turing had been born in 1912 and was probably the greatest mathematician of his age. He was also a massive influence in the development of computer science, inventing something called the

Turing machine, a forerunner of today's PCs.

During World War II he worked at the famous Bletchley Park code breaking centre and invented a series of methods for cracking Germany's infamous Enigma machine. As a result, Turing was acknowledged as the forefather of computing. At the end of the millennium, *Time* magazine listed him among the one hundred most important people of the twentieth century. 'Everyone who taps at a keyboard . . . is working on an incarnation of a Turing machine,' the article said.

Yet Turing's life was destroyed when he was prosecuted for being homosexual in 1952. Homosexuality was against the law at the time. Not only that, but it was considered a mental illness to be treated. Rather than going to prison Turing agreed to be treated with injections of hormones. He committed suicide by taking cyanide in 1954, a few weeks before his forty-second birthday.

It was only in September 2009, after a long internet campaign, that the then Prime Minister Gordon Brown issued a public apology on behalf of the British Government.

I'd come into contact with other well known personalities from history before but this particular connection haunted me for a while afterwards. Alan Turing left this life a tormented and tortured soul. It was good to know that his spirit had found peace and that, on that one night at least, he continued to provide inspiration.

'It is the secret of the world that all things subsist and do not die, but only retire a little from sight and afterwards return again. Nothing is dead; men feign themselves dead, and endure mock funerals . . . and there they stand looking out of the window, sound and well, in some strange new disguise.' RALPH WALDO EMERSON

Finishing The Mural

There are times when it takes the intervention of those who have passed over to the spirit dimension to remind those they have left behind that life must go on.

On more occasions than I can count I've seen wives, husbands, sons, daughters and friends trapped by their grief, seemingly unable to pick up the pieces after the loss of a loved one. Ultimately, no one can do the job for them. Whenever I encounter someone who says to me, 'Oh, I'll never get over the loss of my husband,' my reply is always the same: 'No, with that attitude, you probably won't.' We all need to draw back the curtains and re-engage with the world at some stage after a bereavement.

But there are occasionally times when the spirit world itself intervenes. That's precisely what happened one evening a few years ago when I delivered a very emotional message at a demonstration in a theatre in London.

Towards the end of the first half of the show I felt myself in the presence of a young boy, no older than twenty years of age. I got the sense that he hadn't passed over very long before. I also sensed the name Duncan.

He was directing me towards the balcony of the theatre. It was there that I located a lady.

'Do you understand the name Duncan?' I asked

her.

'Yes, he was my adopted son,' she replied. When he was a toddler he had been accepted into her family as if he was her own. She clearly loved him very much.

'He's showing me a drawing or a painting of parrots,' I said, slightly unsure what it meant.

'That's right,' the lady said. 'He was very artistic and he had started painting a mural of parrots on a wall in our house.'

It was clear from what he was showing me that the mural had remained unfinished.

'Yes, no one has been allowed to touch it since he died,' the lady said. 'We don't know what to do about it. If we get rid of it, it erases our memory of him, but if we let someone else finish the mural it feels like we are disrespecting his memory. We're afraid he would be offended.'

I felt the boy's strength growing after this. He began to show me another boy drawing. 'He is telling me that there is someone in the family who can finish the mural,' I said.

For a moment, the lady looked nonplussed.

'The youngest member of the family,' I added.

She looked shocked now. 'Oh, well yes, he's very gifted as an artist, but he's too young to do that,' she said. 'He isn't ten yet.'

'He's not too young,' I said. 'Duncan is telling me that your youngest boy is now artistically mature enough to finish the mural off.' I smiled. 'Tell him to finish the last parrot.'

It was a highly charged message. The audience was spellbound throughout; many of them were in tears.

As Duncan faded from my consciousness,

however, I felt his happiness. He had succeeded in what he had come along to do. I felt certain that his mural wouldn't remain unfinished for very much longer.

Fashioning The Future

'To live in hearts we leave behind is not to die.' THOMAS CAMPBELL

I've been extremely fortunate in my career to have staged demonstrations at some of the finest theatres in this and other countries. But if I had to pick a personal highlight it would have to be the night I played at the London Palladium.

It was a magical night for several reasons. First and foremost, to stand on the stage that Judy Garland and all the showbusiness greats had stood on was something that was beyond my wildest dreams. But it was also a magical night because of the audience, one of the most receptive and encouraging I've ever worked with.

Unsurprisingly there were several great messages that night. One in particular sticks in my memory. Again it was an example of the spirit world providing the inspiration that was needed for someone who had been left behind here on this earthly plane.

I was in the presence of an elderly man who was directing me towards a young girl somewhere in the audience. I quickly located her, towards the front of the auditorium. She was a pretty young woman, probably in her mid-twenties.

It was clear I had her dad with me. 'I've got your father with me. And he keeps on showing me fashion designs by Stella McCartney,' I said.

She smiled at this but didn't say anything.

Her father then showed me her working on the design of a dress and sitting at a sewing machine. 'You're studying fashion design,' I said.

At this she just nodded and answered: 'Yes.'

'Are you understanding the significance of Stella McCartney?' I wondered.

This time she was a bit more forthcoming. 'She's one of my inspirations—I love her work. In my sketches I try to emulate her style,' she said.

I almost felt a prickling on my skin at this. Her father was clearly so proud of his daughter, although I got the strong sense he hadn't told her so before his passing. He was intent on correcting that.

'Your father wants to tell you that you must not give up,' I said. 'You must persist and follow your ambitions. He didn't follow his dreams during his life but you can do so, not just for yourself but for him too.'

She was crying by now but I could see the determination forming on her face.

'I was thinking of quitting the course,' she admitted. 'But I won't, I won't give in.'

At the end of the show she came to see me. It turned out the message was extremely significant for her.

She had come to the show as a sceptic. 'I always wanted to believe but there's been a part of me that couldn't really,' she told me.

She had desperately wanted to hear from her father, however. 'My father didn't pass away very long ago. We had a bit of a strange relationship because he and my mother were separated,' she explained.

'He always wanted me to be well educated and he and my mother had disagreed about the direction I was taking. I thought he disapproved of what I was doing. It was lovely to hear confirmation from him that in fact he approved very much,' she said.

Whenever I flick through a fashion magazine or see some item about new designers on the television, I look out for her face or her name. I haven't seen it yet, but I have a feeling that one day I will.

5.

HOW THE SPIRITS CAN BRING YOU JOY

'Ancient Egyptians believed that upon death they would be asked two questions and their answers would determine whether they could continue their journey in the afterlife. The first question was, "Did you bring joy?" The second was, "Did you find joy?"' Leo Buscaglia

One of the most common misconceptions about the spirit dimension is that it's a rather sombre, serious place. In my experience, that's simply not true. Just as humour is one of the most important parts of the human experience in this life, so it is in the afterlife.

The key thing you need to remember is that the loved one who passes over doesn't change in character or personality when they reach the other side. Over a long period of time, there is a levelling-out of the personality. But in essence the person remains the same on that side of life as they did in this life. If they were funny, energetic personalities when they were alive, they remain the same on the other side. And vice versa.

I've seen many examples of the humour that exists within the spirit world during the course of my career.

Spaghetti Bolognese

I was performing a demonstration a few years ago in

a small hall in Scotland. Towards the end of the evening I felt myself in the presence of a woman. 'I have a lady with me, her name is Margaret-Anne,' I said. 'The first thought she is putting through to me is that she can see clearly now.'

This didn't mean anything to me but fortunately it did mean something to someone else and an arm shot up in the middle of the theatre.

'I think that's our mum,' the middle-aged woman said, nodding towards the two people either side of her. 'Her name was Margaret-Anne and that's what everyone called her.'

They turned out to be three siblings who had come along together. All three of them looked a bit taken aback that she'd come through.

'Do you understand what she means when she says she can see clearly now?' I asked.

'Yes, we do,' the lady said. 'Our mother was blind from a young age.'

As I communicated further with her, Margaret-Anne showed me an image from when she was a little girl. She must have been a toddler when she lost her sight.

'The only colour she remembers seeing is blue. She remembers one summer's day lying in a chair or a cot and looking up at this perfect blue sky,' I said.

'But now I know what all the colours are,' she said.

This produced a huge smile from her children. 'Thank you, Colin,' the sister said. 'It means a lot to know that.'

This is always a source of huge consolation to those who have lost loved ones who had disabilities of some kind in this life. When they reach the spirit world these disabilities disappear. They lead the same kind of existence as everyone else who has passed over to the spirit dimension.

The three siblings were very relaxed and happy, and the atmosphere in the theatre was very warm and supportive that evening. As is often the case, this was reflected in the message. Margaret-Anne went on to recount a very funny story.

Even though she'd been blind most of her life, she'd had a very successful marriage. Her husband, Michael, had been partially sighted. Margaret-Anne's energy became quite playful and light-hearted as she began to tell me a story about how they used to cook together.

'Even though I was blind and he was partially sighted we came up with a system,' she said. 'He could see the shapes of the pans on the cooker so he used to guide me over to them. I had a very developed sense of smell which allowed me to add the ingredients until things were ready,' she said.

Amazingly, it had worked throughout their long and happy marriage.

There was, however, one occasion when it hadn't been quite so successful. Margaret-Anne told me that one of the family favourites was spaghetti bolognese. She used to make the bolognese sauce, Michael would boil the pasta and then together they'd serve it up.

On this one occasion, however, things didn't quite go to plan.

Over the years Michael and Margaret-Anne had worked out a system for draining the pasta. He would take the colander to the sink and then she would position the saucepan containing the spaghetti over the colander. When he said 'tip now' she would pour the contents of the saucepan into the colander and—hey pasta!—they were in business.

On this particular night, however, they were a little out of synch with each other. As Margaret-Anne held the pan over the sink, Michael placed his colander in position as usual. Unfortunately he got his bearings wrong and placed it in the corner of the large sink, not—as usual—over the plughole.

When Michael said 'tip now' Margaret-Anne emptied the saucepan and the spaghetti flew straight into the sink. As if this wasn't bad enough, the sink had a very wide plughole and there was no grate in it. The spaghetti went straight down the plughole.

As Margaret-Anne recounted this story her three children were in stitches laughing.

Now there might be some people who would think this was inappropriate. 'There you have this tragic family with blind parents. Those children must have missed out on so much in life. How can there be anything funny about that?' they would say.

They would, of course, be completely wrong.

This was clearly an incredibly close family. And one of the reasons they remained close—in death and in life—was that they understood the importance of humour. Goodness knows, there must have been times when their life was almost unbearably hard. But they got through it by understanding that sometimes you had to laugh, not cry.

The children had retained that philosophy after their parents' passing. They had maintained the spirit that had kept their family together. And in so doing they had kept their parents' spirits close by.

It was a wonderful message—and a great lesson for us all.

In The Mood

Humour is incredibly important in our lives. And it can be important at the end of our lives too.

One of the funniest epitaphs ever written was Spike Milligan's: 'I told you I was ill.' Just thinking about it conjures up immediately the madcap, anarchic and extremely funny spirit of the man. It keeps that spirit alive.

A friend of mine provided me with a great example of this many years ago. He had been an acquaintance of Spike Milligan and some of the other Goons and had heard this story about the death of Peter Sellers.

Apparently, during his life Sellers had absolutely hated the music of Glenn Miller. In particular, he had loathed with a passion the song 'In The Mood'.

When Sellers died, at an early age, his three partners from the Goons—Spike, Harry Secombe and Michael Bentine—went along to the memorial service.

The minister at the service was rather solemn and the mood generally was very sad.

The service was drawing to an end when the minister said he wanted to play a piece of music. 'I know this song must have meant a great deal to Peter because he specifically asked for it to be played at his funeral,' he said.

Suddenly the sound of 'In The Mood' by Glenn

Miller started to fill the air inside the church.

The three fellow Goons seemed to be the only people who were in on the joke. They apparently sat there chewing their handkerchiefs in an attempt to stop themselves bursting out laughing.

When he was alive Peter had said that he hated that tune so much that he would have it played at his funeral. 'It will be the one time I can inflict it on everyone else without having to listen to it myself,' he said.

It was a very funny—but also a very profound—gesture. At a moment of sadness for those he loved, he had ensured that the spirit of happiness and joy which had defined his life continued beyond the grave. To me it seemed a perfect send-off.

A Dog Wearing Sunglasses

During a demonstration to an audience in the northeast of England one evening a few years ago, I received a connection from a young woman called Sally.

Sally had passed over during her early thirties—I sensed from breast cancer. She was a very lively, effervescent personality. She had clearly been a fun-loving person in this life. She was no different on the other side.

Sally directed me towards a young woman of about her age who was sitting near the back of the audience. She was showing me the name Jennifer or Jenny.

When I asked the young woman whether the name Sally meant anything to her she nodded. 'I had a good friend called Sally,' she said.

'And the name Jennifer or Jenny?'

'That's my name; I'm Jenny.'

When I asked Jenny whether any of the other information made sense to her, she nodded.

'She died of breast cancer when she was in her early thirties,' she said.

The realisation that I had her friend with me had an immediate impact on her and she became very tearful. Rather than offering words of comfort or consolation, however, Sally was determined to provoke another reaction in her old friend.

'This is going to sound very strange,' I said. 'But she is showing me a big, yellow dog with a pair of sunglasses on.'

The moment I said this Jenny's tears were mixed with a burst of laughter. 'Oh my God!' she said.

Sally went on to show me an incident that had happened years earlier. She, Jenny and some other friends had gone out for lunch one day in their local market town. It had been a very jolly affair, as it often was when they got together. They had had a couple of bottles of wine and were in extremely high spirits when they left the restaurant.

They had come across one of the Golden Labrador-shaped collection boxes that the Royal National Institute for the Blind used to leave outside shops. This one was outside the town's post office.

It had been Sally who had suggested picking it up and taking the dog for a walk around town, and Jenny had been her chief partner in crime. One of them had a camera and they proceeded to take photographs of the dog in various locations. It was a beautiful summer's day and they were both wearing sunglasses and hats.

They couldn't resist dressing the dog up for one final picture before returning the collection box.

They'd never intended to do anything wrong with the collection box. In fact they'd put some money into it. And when they finished their little tour of the town they returned it to the post office. Unfortunately, when they arrived there they discovered a police officer waiting for them.

Reports of their rather tipsy behaviour had been coming in from all over the town. They'd been seen carrying the dog with them.

For a moment the two had been really worried they would be arrested. But when they explained what had happened they escaped with nothing worse than a severe telling-off from the policeman.

By the time we'd recounted this story, the whole audience were in hysterics. For Jenny it was all excruciatingly embarrassing. The episode had obviously been completely out of character. As I recounted the tale that Sally was telling me, I could see her sliding slowly down into her chair. It was as if she wanted the earth to swallow her up.

She came up to me afterwards. 'I want to thank you, Colin,' she said. 'At first all I could think about when Sally came through was how tragic it was that she wasn't around any more. She'd have loved to have been with us tonight.'

'But she was here,' I said.

'Exactly,' Jenny said. 'And she did what she always did when she was alive—she put a smile on my face. That was her gift. So thank you for reminding me of that.'

It was a lovely moment, one that stayed with me for a long time afterwards. I often get communications like that, in which spirits come through to me simply to cheer up their friends and loved ones when they are feeling low.

Their message is invariably the same: 'Don't be sad for me: apart from that little bit of tragedy at the end, I had a good life and you should remember it and celebrate it with a smile.'

'I believe that when death closes our eyes we shall awaken to a light, of which our sunlight is but the shadow.' ARTHUR SCHOPENHAUER

Russell's Smile

I meet a lot of people who complain about their lives. They come to me often to ask the spirit of a loved one to help them find happiness. Invariably they are disappointed. The truth is that true happiness lies within you. It isn't for someone else to give it to you.

I always try to offer people who feel disenchanted or miserable about their lives some perspective. During the course of our lives, every single person will experience sadness, joy, depression and disappointment. But not every day of our lives will be sad, joyless, depressing or disappointing. Far from it, in fact. When you sit back on a normal day you have to be able to acknowledge that there is more good in your life than bad.

Things could be a lot worse. And very often I tell people a little story that illustrates this point.

When I was in my early twenties, I devoted a fair amount of my time to working with charities. I supported the Samaritans and I was also a volunteer on the Brighton gay switchboard. In addition I helped out at a local charity in Sussex caring for people with severe disabilities.

One morning each week I used to go and help out at a school for mentally handicapped children. Some of them also had quite terrible physical disabilities.

I remember one little lad who was severely mentally handicapped and also severely physically handicapped. His name was Russell and he had an acute form of spondylitis which affected his spine. It really was a terrible condition. It was so bad he couldn't sit or be positioned normally. In effect, he was always curled up in a ball.

That was how I'd find him on a Wednesday morning. He'd be in a big beanbag, coiled up in this foetal position. The amazing thing was that he wouldn't be there crying or complaining of the pain he must have been in. He'd be lying there smiling.

I was twenty-one or so at the time and I remember thinking to myself, 'What on earth have I got to feel unhappy about it in life?' And it was true.

We all whinge and we all moan about things going on in our life. We all feel sorrow about the people coming to the end of their lives. But here was this young boy who, because of the condition of his spine, was never going to experience many of the simple pleasures that we all take for granted.

He was about eight at the time but he wasn't given more than another three or four years to live. One of the carers said to me that this condition meant that eventually his spine would snap and he would die. His organs were gradually getting crushed. It was an awful thing to witness. And yet Russell smiled and giggled all the time.

Just as his carers predicted, Russell passed away at the age of ten or so. I wanted to go to his funeral but was committed to something else at the time. But I took some time to think about him that day. And I've thought about him often in the years that have passed too, as I'm sure everyone who came into contact with him does.

The thing all of us will remember is his smile. We won't remember this physically handicapped boy. We won't remember the distorted figure lying in the beanbag. All we'll remember is that beaming, beautiful smile.

Over the years I have had communications from people who had severe handicaps. It is always a great source of comfort to those they have left behind that they are free of the pain they suffered in this earthly existence.

Whenever I do receive a message like that I always think of Russell. And I always think of his smile.

6.

HOW THE SPIRITS CAN GUIDE YOU

'The power of the Spirit is the power of life. The reason why there is life is because Spirit is there. The power that fashioned the whole universe, majestic though it is and stupendously vast, is the same power which enables you to exist here and hereafter for all time.' SILVER BIRCH

The spirit world is at work guiding us at all times. Sometimes it works in an obvious and highly visible way. Most of the time, however, it is busy steering us through the choppy and complicated waters of our lives quietly and invisibly.

During the course of my career I have benefited from its silent hand many times. So too have the many people whom I have put in touch with the spirit dimension.

The Ring Of Truth

Spirit communication is a controversial subject in many places. From my travels around the world, I know that the interest in it is pretty much universal, crossing all boundaries and all faiths. But it is not always a subject that can be talked about openly.

Some formal religions, for instance, disapprove of mediums and actively discourage their followers from visiting them for personal readings or even going to see demonstrations. This is something that, I believe, dates back to ancient, pre-Christian times and a power struggle that has long gone on between organised religion and those who are gifted with unusual powers, such as mediums.

The irony is that that the major organised religions are all deeply interested in the subject— as I know from personal experience. A couple of examples that underline this spring to mind.

Several years ago I visited Ireland to put on a series of demonstrations in some theatres there. Despite the fact that the Catholic Church, which is still a dominant voice in the life of ordinary Irish people, had been disapproving of mediums, the theatres were all full.

One night I staged a demonstration in Dublin. It went well and afterwards, as is often the case, a long queue of people formed to buy copies of my books, ask me to pose for photographs and to say hello.

I looked up at one point and noticed that standing patiently in line, looking slightly nervous, were three ladies with short haircuts, dressed in what I can only describe as Oxfam dresses. With them was a gentleman wearing a very ill-fitting suit.

It was so obvious who they were.

As they arrived at the front of the queue, I smiled and said: 'Good evening, Sisters; good evening, Father'.

For a moment they looked at me, mildly shocked. 'How did you know?' one of them whispered.

I didn't have the heart to tell them the way they were dressed was a complete giveaway, so I simply said: 'Well, I am psychic!'

They were absolutely charming people and we chatted for a little while. As we did so, one of the nuns leaned over conspiratorially towards me and whispered, 'You know, we're not supposed to be here.'

'I bet you're not,' I said.

They went on to tell me that they watched my television show *6ixth Sense* in the convent with the priest. 'It's our little guilty secret,' she said.

The memory of that encounter returned to me a year or so later, when, back at home in England, I was contacted by a gentleman who wanted a private sitting with me.

I didn't do that many private sittings at the time but there was something about the man's voice that intrigued me. When he turned up he was quite a distinguished-looking man, dressed in a smart, pinstripe suit. He was in his late fifties or possibly his early sixties. He was very polite but not particularly talkative. I didn't think too much of it and began the reading as usual.

We hadn't been sitting for long when I felt myself in the presence of a nun. Now, nuns are often spirit guides but this was definitely not a guide. It was the spirit of lady who had lived in a convent until quite recently.

'In life you knew this lady,' I told the man. I went on to describe her. I described how she had maintained a very sharp mind throughout her life, but that in her final years she became crippled with arthritis.

I felt the reading was a very strong and accurate one, but there was no feedback from the man. In fact, he didn't respond at all. He simply sat there, unblinking, listening to what I had to say.

The nun was very communicative and continued to tell me about her relationship with this man. 'I know she was a huge influence on your life,' I said. 'She is showing me that she had a lot to do with your education and training.'

Again he acknowledged nothing, and simply sat in silence.

'She is telling me that you will come and see me again, but that you will not come on your own next time, you will come with someone else,' I said.

There were various other bits and pieces of information, but that was essentially the message. At the end of the reading, the man simply got up, said, 'Thank you very much,' shook my hand, paid his fee and left.

'What a strange sitting,' I thought to myself afterwards. I don't think I'd ever come across someone so uncommunicative and someone who had remained so unmoved by a reading.

To my surprise, a couple of days later I picked up the phone to discover the man's distinguished-sounding voice on the end of the line once more. 'Mr Fry, I'd like to come and see you again—and I'd like to bring a friend with me this time,' he said.

I smiled at this. I had believed the nun when she predicted that he would come to see me again but I hadn't expected it to happen quite so quickly.

'You're more than welcome,' I said, before finding room in my diary for these mysterious visitors. I must admit I was very intrigued.

He showed up a week or so later with another man. This one was, like him, wearing a very smart suit. He was also carrying a briefcase which he put down next to him.

To my surprise the same nun came through, this

time directing her messages to the new man.

'She's showing me that you have a letter in the briefcase,' I said.

'But you also have a ring that you should be wearing and aren't.'

Like his colleague, the man said nothing. He just sat there blank-faced. Then, completely out of the blue, the nun placed a powerful single image in my mind.

'You're a cardinal,' I said. 'It's your papal ring that you're not wearing.

'She's asking me to tell you she hopes that, whatever the letter inside your briefcase says, you are now answered to your satisfaction.'

It was one of those readings where I never quite understood the implications of what I was saying or being asked to say.

Throughout, they kept looking at each other with quite shocked expressions.

Sure enough at the end one of them introduced himself as a cardinal from the Vatican. 'We do hope we haven't offended you,' he said. 'But you may not understand the wider significance of our visit and what has been done here.

'We have been given the task of examining the gifts of people such as yourself. The nun that you are claiming to be communicating with was known to both of us,' he said.

The other man was a priest and the nun had been one of the tutors at the seminary where he studied.

It turned out that the whole thing was part of a major investigation to see whether there was anything in what we were doing. I also discovered later that several other well-known mediums both in the UK and in America had had the same experience. They'd received out-of-the-blue requests to sit for these anonymous men.

They were far from the first members of an organised religion to come to see me. The need to feel connected to the people who have passed over to the other side of life is universal and I have had people from all faiths come to sittings. Hindu holy men have come to see me to talk about belief and the afterlife. I have done readings for senior members of Royal Families from Muslim countries. I had to be incredibly discreet in those cases as they could have got themselves into a lot of trouble because mediumship is very much frowned upon by Islam.

It was very strange because soon after the cardinal's visit I heard through a very reliable source that the Roman Catholic Church had subtly changed its ruling about whether members could consort with mediums. I haven't seen any direct proof of this, but apparently the then pope, John Paul II, had moderated the ruling to say you could see a medium provided they were Catholic and you were in the presence of a priest.

I have no doubt that the spirit world was working together in unison to orchestrate this. They had guided these men at this time towards me. And they in turn had been given the guidance they were looking for.

I have believed for many years that Spiritualism has the potential to be a uniting factor that can bring together all faiths and beliefs. But religions have to strive to recognise the similarities they share and not dwell on the perceived differences that divide them.

Carrying On

The spirits are extremely determined and persistent forces. When they set their collective mind on something, they will do whatever is necessary to make it happen. For instance, if they aren't able to make direct contact with someone on this earthly plane they will regularly use someone else to pass on their communications.

So it proved when, one night while sitting in my regular circle, we were contacted by the late, great comic Kenneth Williams.

Like most members of my generation, I remembered him best for his roles in the 'Carry On' films. His most famous line, 'Infamy, infamy, they've all got it in for me,' was voted the funniest in cinema history in a poll, and quite right too.

So when he came through at a regular weekly meeting of our circle one evening no one was surprised when he was very amusing. That famously dry, caustic, camp wit of his shone through, apparently.

But his communication was also very serious and moving. As many people know, Kenneth Williams's private life was far from a barrel of laughs. He was a lonely man who failed to find personal happiness in a relationship and, in a way, cut himself off from the rest of the world. He committed suicide by taking an overdose of barbiturates. His mother, to whom he was very close, died soon afterwards, leaving his sister.

Understanding and dealing with the loss of a loved one to suicide is very difficult. The normal emotions of grief and loss are intermingled with feelings of confusion, guilt and often anger. His sister had been devastated at her brother's death but had kept a dignified silence in public.

It seems that Kenneth knew the pain he'd caused his sister.

When he came through he said that he wanted to be able to get a message to her. 'I need to explain to her what I did,' he said. 'I need her to know why I left her here.'

It had been our circle leader who had explained to him, as gently as possible, that it was going to be difficult because we didn't have any connections to his sister. 'How would we get in touch with her?' he asked.

Apparently Kenneth was quite determined and insisted that, after the circle had broken, we somehow make contact with a friend of his, a lady called Carol Hawkins. Our circle leader had said he would do his best.

The atmosphere was quite lively after the circle broke up. We had had connections to well known people before but there was a real sense of us having been given a mission in this case. We all agreed that we needed to try to make contact with Carol Hawkins, whoever she might be.

'Do you know, I think I realise who Carol Hawkins is. Wasn't she the actress who used to be in that TV comedy series *Please Sir!*?' one member said.

'That's right,' I said.

As I say, the spirit world has a way of making things happen. Sure enough, a few days after Kenneth Williams had come through, our circle leader got a phone call from a mutual friend of the circle. 'I've just had a phone call from a friend of the medium Leslie Flint's. She's an actress, you might remember her from *Please Sir!* years ago, her name is Carol Hawkins,' she'd said. She continued, 'She says she'd like to come along and sit in Colin's circle because she's heard about him.'

Our circle leader was stunned. When he recovered his composure he explained.

'Well, actually,' he said, 'we've already been told to invite her along to the circle by a friend of hers who I can't name at the moment,' he said. 'He wants to speak to her.'

So it was that Carol Hawkins came along to join our circle the following week. She came with her husband and they took their places in the group as I went into a trance.

Kenneth came through again and spoke to Carol. He explained that life had become very hard for him. He had been due to have an operation for a stomach ulcer and was suffering terribly from depression. He also repeated something he had said when he was alive, that he didn't see any point in living beyond his mid-sixties. 'I always said "why hang around?" and I meant it,' he said.

His only regret was knowing how much pain and upset he'd caused his family. His mother, who had lived in a flat almost next door to his in central London, had passed over a short time after Kenneth. His sister had been left behind to deal with the publicity and rumours that had swirled around Kenneth's death. She had found it hard to cope with but Kenneth wanted Carol to tell her he appreciated all she had done.

'She was a good sister and she was as protective of me in death as she was in life,' he said.

Carol was really moved by the communication. After the circle broke up she took me to one side and said she was stunned at how accurate it was.

Apparently Kenneth, through me, had repeated the last conversation they had had together. 'Colin, it was accurate, word for word,' she said. 'I remember it so vividly. We'd been driving home after doing a play together. It was the last time I saw him,' she said.

Carol went on to let friends know that Kenneth had come through. His sister may also have found out about his message. Regardless, I knew that on that one night an old friend had been very happy to hear from him.

SPIRIT SECRET
About seventy per cent of the communications I receive come from direct members of a person's family or close friends who were well known to the recipient of the message. The other thirty per cent are made up of friends and acquaintances, but also complete strangers. Often these strangers are bearing the most powerful messages of all.

Completing The Circle

In many ways my development as a medium owed everything to the spirit world. Without its regular intervention I wouldn't have been able to learn what I did as a younger man. Not only did the spirits lead me to Geraldine and John, the people who would oversee my development. They then made sure that, whenever we needed to keep my development circle going, suitable people turned up.

To begin with it was just me, John and

Geraldine meeting in the room in Hove where I'd first brought through their son. We'd also been joined by a lovely old fellow called Lenny.

As I developed as a trance medium, however, the guides kept saying to me: 'You need more people for this circle in case people come and go.' However, it was very difficult to get people to come along and sit for the development of another medium, which was me. But the guides kept saying, 'They will come.'

One day a guide said while I was in trance, 'There is a lady who is known to the medium who will join the circle.'

When John told me this I said, 'I don't have a clue who they're talking about.'

At the time I had a part-time job in a local pub. I used to run the pub on a Thursday evening for these friends so that they could have a night off. All of a sudden my mum came in with a friend of hers, a lady called Pat, whom I hadn't seen in years. We'd always got on really well.

'Your mum tells me that you're sitting in a circle,' she said.

'That's right,' I said. 'I started only a few weeks ago.'

'That's weird,' she said. 'Because I've just had a reading at the College of Psychic Studies. A medium up there told me I should join a circle.'

'Now I know who they were talking about,' I said to myself. 'Yes, come along,' I told her. 'See what you think.'

She was soon a regular member of the circle.

Pat then said she knew a young lady, the daughter of a friend, who would be perfect.

The guides said no.

'Why not?—she'd be perfect,' she insisted.

'She would be perfect,' the guides said. 'But she can't join for a year.'

I said, 'I can't explain but it will soon become apparent.'

Within a few days of this, the girl, whose name was Justine, went down with glandular fever. She was quite unwell for about nine months. When she recovered the guides said she was now ready to be invited into the circle.

At that point the guides said we needed one more person. Although we knew each other quite well within the circle, we didn't socialise with each other outside. We didn't know anything about each other's families, apart from me and Pat through my mum.

After a while Pat said to Justine, 'Why don't you invite your partner to come along?'

Justine looked surprised. 'Oh no, he's not interested in this.'

Pat said to invite him anyway as a guest.

He came along and during the circle one of the guides asked him if he wanted to stay on.

Much to Justine's surprise he said yes. And he became the fifth sitter. The five of us then sat for eleven years, every Tuesday night. Without the intervention of the spirits, that would never have happened and I would never have developed my mediumship skills further.

A Helping Hand

Being in close contact with the spirit world can be very useful at times. I've mentioned that during my early days as a medium, when I was still working in other jobs, I spent some time behind the bar of a local pub. I rather enjoyed the work; it was very sociable and friendly, and I made some good acquaintances.

I remember one Saturday evening when I finished at the pub for the night, I asked a bunch of the guys and girls I knew well to come back to my house for a drink. I was in a good mood and felt like winding down from my night's work with a glass of wine and some good company.

They were a fun group. None of them was connected to my mediumship although they all knew I was involved in the Spiritualist Church and was rumoured to have 'a gift'.

Everyone was in high spirits when we got back to my house and I opened a few bottles of wine. As we chatted a couple of the girls quite light-heartedly started taking the mickey out of what I did as a medium.

'One of your spirits must have told you we were going to come back tonight,' one of them joked. 'Otherwise you wouldn't have had some wine ready for us.'

I didn't react strongly even though I did find it slightly disrespectful. 'You really shouldn't mock the spirits, you know. If you put them to the test they'll do something that will surprise you,' I warned.

The girls' eyes lit up at this. 'Go on, Colin, make something happen then,' one of them said.

Again it was irritating to hear someone who clearly knew nothing about what I did making silly comments. But once more I bit my lip. 'I don't make things happen. Things happen according to their will, not mine. It's up to them.'

During this time in my development, I always felt Magnus's presence was around me. He was very much fulfilling his role as my guide, overseeing my progress as a medium.

As I poured the girls a glass of wine, I just put a thought out to Magnus. 'I'm in a spot here, I need to be able to defend you and what you do with me and through me,' I said. 'Can you help?'

Once everyone had a drink we went into the living room. At the time I used to smoke. (I'm glad to say I've quit now!) Anyway, I had lit up a cigarette and there was a large round coffee table that everyone was sitting around. 'Could someone pass me the ashtray?' I asked.

'Of course, Colin,' one of the girls said, leaning over to reach for the large, glass ashtray I had on the table.

But before she or anyone else could touch it, it suddenly slid quite quickly right across the table towards me on its own.

That shut them up. I will never forget the look on their faces.

'Colin, what the heck was that?' one of them gasped.

'Oh, just Magnus. He's always doing little things like that,' I said with a playful smile.

'That's too weird,' one of the guys said, shaking his head.

'I did warn you,' I said.

We continued to have a fun night and carried on talking and drinking into the small hours. But no one made light of my mediumship again that night. Or indeed ever again.

A Spirit A to Z

The spirit world can help you in all sorts of ways. It can offer advice on the most profound and important matters in your life, but it can also help you with the most mundane little things too.

It can, for instance, act as a glorified tourist information centre, as I once discovered when I visited Australia.

I had flown Down Under to undertake some public demonstrations in a few major cities, including Melbourne. It was my first tour of Australia. I was working hard, six days a week, Tuesday to Sunday with only Mondays off. I did this for four weeks.

My manager of the time and I spent this particular Monday off together. We were staying about twenty miles outside Melbourne, so that day we asked to be dropped off at a station called Lilydale, and we caught a train into the city.

I was something of a man on a mission that day. I am a great collector of antiquarian books, especially books on spiritualism and mediumship. I have a large collection of them at home. Before flying down to Australia I'd been told by another book collector that there was a particularly good shop in Melbourne that often had very rare and old spiritualist books. The collector had given me the name and the address of the shop.

Now I had never been to this city before and I hadn't had time to even look at a map of Melbourne in advance of arriving there. So when we disembarked at Melbourne's central station and headed out into the streets, my first port of call should have been a tourist information centre or a bookstore selling street maps.

Yet I didn't need either. It was the most curious feeling—I knew exactly where I was.

'OK,' I said to my then manager, 'we head left down here and walk along for about a quarter of a mile until we reach a junction. From there we need to follow a winding street down the hill until we find a little street off that. The bookshop is on the far corner.'

He just looked at me as if I'd lost my mind. 'How do you know that?' he wondered. 'You've looked at a map, haven't you?'

'No I haven't,' I said. 'I have no idea why or how, but I can see it all as clearly as anything in my mind.'

Sure enough, when we followed the directions I'd somehow had imprinted or embedded in my head, they led us straight to the bookshop. And it was every bit as much of a treasure trove as I'd hoped. I spent a little too much money in there, that's for sure.

It was only later that night, as my manager and I sat down and had a glass of wine in the hotel bar, that we thought about possible explanations. Neither of us particularly believed in reincarnation.

'I'm pretty sure I've not had a previous life in Australia,' I said. I'd also experienced remote viewing in the past, a phenomenon where I suddenly had the ability to see something from afar. But it didn't feel like that at all.

Instead it was as if knowledge of this place had been implanted in my mind.

I quite often talk to Magnus when I go to bed or have a bath.

'Come on Magnus, what was that all about?' I asked him that night.

There are times when he will not divulge how he has done something. He will simply stay silent. On this occasion, however, he was more forthcoming. 'I knew you'd get hopelessly lost,' he said. 'So I found the information and implanted it in your mind for you.'

It was as if he had downloaded an *A to Z* into my head. It was an amazing experience.

Free Will

Faith and belief are wonderful things. But they are also precious things that should not be abused or used for the purposes of removing people's free will.

Faith and belief aren't so wonderful when they allow people to say things like: 'We will take away responsibility for you to think for yourself' or 'You don't have to worry about what to think, we will tell you what to think' or 'What we tell you to believe is absolute and you must not sway from it.'

That's not faith or belief—that's dictatorship, and I am sad for those people who would blindly give up free will to adopt that attitude. They are living in a fool's paradise.

We all have to think for ourselves, we all have to learn for ourselves. When you learn to cook you may have to burn yourself on the oven door a few times before the penny drops and you realise you should wear oven gloves. We are human beings and we were given free will and a mind to analyse and sort things out for ourselves.

I have made mistakes and I will make many more. It is my free will to get it right or wrong.

Guides and other influences have certainly helped me to expand my knowledge. One of the things that I've learned is that my guide will not give me all the answers. The spirit world has not protected me: it has encouraged me to go out and take the risk that I might get my fingers burned. But the good news is that it has taught me that I am strong, not weak.

The spirits have at times given me the tools but I have to take on the task. Magnus once told me he could take me to the greatest library in the universe but I would still have to read the books and without enough life experience I wouldn't even understand most of them.

SPIRIT SECRET

Spirits aren't infallible. The spirit world reinforces many of the lessons we learn in this earthly life. For instance, it underlines the importance of positive thinking and of being of service to others. But it also confirms other, subtler points about life here on the earthly plane.

One thing I have learned during my thirty years and more working as a medium is that there are times when you should listen to the advice of spirits. But there are also times when you should still act according to your own thinking.

This is something that people find surprising.

People often make me smile privately when they say that I am lucky because 'I always have my guide to sort things out for me'. People seem to imagine, I think, that I don't step out of my front door without asking my guide what to do. They imagine that I won't set foot in the supermarket until I have checked with the spirits on whether I should be shopping today. Some people probably even think they dictate my shopping list!

How ridiculous.

People often ask me whether spirits are infallible. The answer is absolutely not.

So when spirit communicators or guides come through to me from the other side of life, whatever they say to me personally I will weigh up but then I will make my own decision. I may well be influenced by what they have said. But I'm certainly not going to let them make decisions for me. I'm not going to let their advice be an absolute answer to every situation.

This is something that everyone should bear in mind.

Quite often people have this highly romanticised view of spirit communications. There is no doubt that they are special communications. But we have to guard against hoping they will give absolute answers when things are going wrong in this life.

Sadly, as I look at the world, it is not just religion that wants to dictate what we should think. Government and the scientific community are just as guilty. In earthly life and spirit life, if you completely give up your free will and your ability to think for yourself someone or something will—rightly or wrongly—do your thinking for you. And you will have lost control of the one thing that is eternal—yourself.

A Move In The Wrong Direction

All too often people come along to a reading or a public demonstration hoping that their mum or their dad or someone who was very important to them will come through and tell them what to do in life.

But are they always right to place such great store in their advice? Perhaps not. Before people listen to a piece of specific advice delivered in a spirit communication I sometimes ask them to ask themselves a few simple questions.

Would you have taken that much notice of their opinion in this life? Would you have listened if they had told you to do something very specific? In general, in this life do you act on everything that you are told? You might think they've got more life experience to draw on but that's not always the case.

I do think that when people are listening to spirit communication they have to weigh it up carefully.

The personality of the person who has passed over doesn't change as soon as they reach the spirit dimension. If they had strong views or prejudices in life, they will still have them in the spirit world until spirit existence shows them otherwise.

So what if, for instance, you had an auntie who didn't like your wife and didn't make a secret of it when she was alive? And what if you had told her to keep her opinions to herself when she was alive?

What if after she'd passed over she came

104

through to give you a message and she told you that you should divorce your wife? Would you listen to her then? Just because that advice is coming through from the other side would you get up and head straight for the solicitor's office? No, of course you wouldn't.

When they pass over, people are not transformed into all-knowing, all-seeing angels with a direct line to God. It just doesn't happen that way. Magnus has said so many times to me and others, 'Judge us by what we say, not what we claim to be.'

I knew a woman who was a medium in her own right whose mother came through to her in a reading. Her mother was quite a bossy type on this side of life and was no different now that she'd passed over. She started telling her daughter that she had to make some changes in her life.

'I think you should move house, move to Wales where we had all those lovely holidays together,' she said.

The daughter was going through a difficult time emotionally and was very affected by the message. To all her friends' horror, she announced that she was leaving her home in the southeast of England and moving to the Welsh countryside.

She sold her very nice property and bought a rundown cottage in a remote part of Wales. And of course she hated it.

She lasted there six months before she decided she'd made the most horrendous mistake. The problem was that she then had a terrible time reversing the process.

By the time she'd sold her cottage in Wales the price of a house in the southeast of England had shot up. She couldn't afford a place the size she'd had previously. She ended up living back in the same area, where she was happier but in a much smaller house.

It was a classic example of someone acting on a message without thinking it through. The crazy thing was that she and her mother clashed all the time when she was alive.

If her mother had given her such advice in this life she would have turned round to her and said, 'Why would I move away from all my friends and family and everything I've got in life? Are you mad?' She'd probably also have told her to stop interfering in her life.

But because it was a communication from the other side of life, she thought the advice was infallible. It wasn't.

Messages are human communications. And for that reason they are open to interpretation. Sometimes it's not that the communication is incorrect; it's how people respond to that information that often defies any sense of reason or logic. This was definitely such a case.

7.

HOW THE SPIRITS CAN ENLIGHTEN YOU

'Nothing that is possible in spirit is impossible
in flesh and blood. Nothing that man can
think is impossible. Nothing that man can
imagine is impossible of realisation.'
WALLACE D WATTLES

A sceptic once said to me: 'How come you've had all
these experiences and I haven't? Why is that?'

'That's easy,' I replied. 'It's because you spend
all your time sitting in front of your computer
screen whinging about the fact that you don't
believe in this and you don't believe in that. But
you aren't going to believe in anything unless you
go out and find the evidence for it.

'The simple fact is that you have to go out and
look for it. Otherwise, it's like someone saying
because I have never seen an elephant I don't
believe they exist. How else are you going to find
the truth?'

During the course of my life, the spirit world has
opened my eyes to remarkable truths—about this
life and the next.

Mr Nikkei's Dragon

I had some very strange experiences when I visited
Japan at the end of the 1990s but none was stranger
than the one that I had with a gentleman called
Mr Nikkei, the chairman of the Japanese Spiritualist

Society.

He was a charming man, incredibly polite and generous, as indeed were most of the people I met there. He was also very elderly and extremely revered within the spiritualist community.

One day our interpreter turned to me and my friend George Cranley, who had accompanied me on the tour, and said: 'Mr Nikkei would like to invite you to his home.'

'Oh yes,' I said.

'Yes,' she continued. 'He would like to show you his spirit photographs of dragons.'

The invitation caught me off guard. Firstly, I was surprised because, as a rule, Japanese people do not invite you to their homes. If you meet, you tend to meet in public places, so we were being greatly honoured by this invitation.

Secondly, I was very wary of being shown something that I might not treat with the proper respect. My Western mind was saying 'Dragons? That's absurd!'

I had seen a number of spirit photographs over the years. The idea of human spirits and even animals being seen next to earthly figures wasn't an alien concept to me. But the idea of seeing dragons was a bit much for me. I agreed to go along but was extremely sceptical.

We arrived at Mr Nikkei's house and took off our shoes, as is the Japanese custom. We were then led into a room with a small, low table and asked to sit on the floor around it.

Mr Nikkei then produced this very large photo album.

I was braced for a disappointment. I really expected to see something that had been created by Photoshop or some other clever computer program.

But when Mr Nikkei opened up the album, I saw image after image of these strange, smoke-shaped, ectoplasmic figures. And there was no question about it: they were images of Oriental-looking dragons.

I have to admit I was completely thrown by this. I've always treated new experiences with an open mind, but I hadn't expected to see such vivid and unquestionably real photographs.

That evening when I went back to the hotel I had to sit down and have a serious think. As I did so I began to realise that spirit communication is very clever. I began to understand that, even though many people may find the concept totally impossible, here the spirit world was manifesting itself according to the belief system of Japan.

For Japanese culture the experience of seeing an image of a dragon is no different to the way in which Western culture experiences angels, guides and guardians. Here, the spirit world was making itself manifest in a way that their minds could acknowledge or accept. The spirit world uses a visual language that respects the culture of the society or individual.

My visit to Mr Nikkei's house taught me some valuable lessons. To begin with it made me more tolerant of belief systems in the world. It made me realise that it is not their job to give us absolute answers; their task is to give us a means of understanding, a way of interpreting and appreciating the mysteries and wonders of this life—and the next one.

Most of all, however, it taught me that, when it

came to the relationship between the physical and the spirit world, absolutely nothing was impossible.

A Painful Separation

People often ask me about the afterlife. They want to know what it looks like, whether they will meet certain people there, what the 'rules' are. I don't claim to know all the answers, but the answers I do have are generally based on details that have been passed on or shown to me by the spirits with whom I have communicated during the course of my career.

Ever since I began practising as a medium, spirits have been providing me with these insights into the afterlife. Sometimes they are the tiniest of details. At other times, they are hugely significant. They all add to the big picture; they are all pieces in the infinite jigsaw puzzle.

One important lesson, for instance, concerned people who take their own lives by committing suicide.

The events leading up to this happened quite early on during my career, when I became friendly with a wealthy lady who lived near me in Sussex.

She was a very grand lady. Her family apparently had aristocratic connections in France. Somehow she had heard about my work and invited me over to her home for a private sitting.

From the start we had got on like a house on fire. It wasn't hard to like her; she was a tremendous character, a woman who was a lot of fun to be around, despite her airs and graces. She would lie draped on a chaise longue while people came in to see her. It was almost like being summoned in to see the Queen.

I read for her for a couple of years. During the early days it was often a great deal of fun. Towards the end, however, she became very seriously ill with cancer and the readings became more sombre. She hadn't told me about her illness but I picked up on it quite quickly.

If I'm honest, I was never quite sure how to approach her when I first did readings with her. I was still a young man and I didn't know how to deal with everything at that age. You can have the gift, but not the life experience. On this occasion, a member of her family came through and I knew immediately what she was showing me.

I remember being quite vague and basically skirting round the issue. She just looked at me and said: 'Darling, I know what you are trying to tell me. Yes, I do have cancer, and I am not going to beat it,' she said. 'Basically I am dying.'

The lady was actually a practising Catholic. As we got to know each other better, I asked her why she took an interest in something that was disapproved of by the Church.

She smiled and looked at me. 'I have upset and offended a lot of people in my life,' she said to me. 'I just want to make sure that the air is cleared between us before I go over.'

After a long and very brave battle she sadly died of cancer. Her death was tragic, but what followed it was even more terrible.

She had been very happily married, but if I'm honest her husband quite frightened me. He was a rather powerful city financier and, truth be told, I don't think he approved of me very much. When I was around he made himself very scarce.

It was quite clear, however, that he was utterly

besotted with his wife, with whom he had three grown-up children. When she died he went to pieces, turning to alcohol to escape the pain he was suffering. What no one knew was that he was also suffering from cancer.

Not very long after her death I heard through some friends that he had committed suicide.

It was a few weeks after his passing that the spirit of his wife came to see me. I was sitting at home one evening when I was suddenly aware that she was in the room with me.

She wasn't in a very good mood.

'What's the matter?' I said.

'I can't be with him,' she said sadly.

'What do you mean?' I asked.

'Because he took his own life, they won't let us be together. I can see him and he can see me but we can't be together because of what he did,' she said.

I was still a relatively young medium at the time—there were many aspects of the afterlife and its workings that were unknown to me. This was a revelation.

She went on to explain that, in effect, her husband had achieved the exact opposite of what he'd hoped to achieve. He'd wanted them to be together again. But by interfering with the natural course of his life in the way he had, he had only succeeded in preventing them from being together.

Her spirit stayed in my presence for quite some time while we talked about it. She said there were spirit guides working very hard to rebalance it to get them back together again. Again this was a fascinating new insight into the machinations of the spirit world.

I was very moved by the communication and couldn't stop thinking about it afterwards. I began to read and re-read some of the classic books on spiritualism and mediumship. I also consulted my guide Magnus who confirmed that what she had told me was true.

The spirit of the lady came back to speak to me a few months later. She was much less agitated this time. Her energy was much calmer. She told me that she and her husband were now back together.

Again she revealed something new to me during the conversation. 'We are together now because this is the time when he would have joined me anyway,' she said. 'He was dying too.'

The lessons I learned from my association with this lady were among the most valuable I acquired during that period in my life. I have used that wisdom more than once to advise people desperate to rejoin their loved ones on the other side against taking their own lives.

Each time I have done so I have seen her face . . .

Raymond

A lot of very important literature has been written about the spirit world, some of it serious investigation.

One of the most important and popular works is a book called *Raymond* written by the scientist Sir Oliver Lodge at the beginning of the last century.

Raymond had been a highly promising boy. He had studied at Birmingham University and was set on a career in science like his father. But, like so many millions of other young men of his

113

generation, his life was transformed with the outbreak of the First World War. He died in the trenches at Ypres.

Sir Oliver was absolutely devastated by the loss of his son. But rather than dwelling on his death in a negative sense, he began a series of scientific investigations into the afterlife.

Eventually Sir Oliver made contact with a medium who was able to channel communications from Raymond. Sir Oliver documented and recorded all of them. They formed the basis for his book, one of the most remarkable and insightful studies into the spirit world I have ever read.

Raymond revealed aspects of the afterlife that I have found to be absolutely true. In particular, he described the afterlife in the most vivid and evocative language. He talked about how, at first, he felt like he was dreaming for weeks when he first passed over.

When he first woke up he felt 'a little depression, but it didn't last long'. He described the afterlife as 'like finding yourself in a strange place, a strange city, with people you hadn't seen, or not seen for a long time round you'.

There was no day and night although he could see the sun constantly. He didn't feel the heat because he 'hasn't got the same body that sensed the heat', he revealed. It was only when he 'comes into contact with the earth plane and is manifesting' that he felt cold although 'not when he comes in the ordinary way just to look round'.

The really interesting thing that I drew from that book when I first read it was how unchanged Raymond was on the other side. One of the reasons his father was persuaded that it really was his beloved son was the way he spoke, the way he sang songs, his general personality.

It's apparent through the communications that Raymond had always been a very kind and sensitive boy when he was on this side. He remained that way on the spirit side. He did not fundamentally become any different a person to what he was in life. And that's something we all need to bear in mind.

A Farewell Poem

There are times when I feel the presence of the spirit so strongly that I begin to take on some of their characteristics. At a demonstration in Surrey one evening a while ago I found myself doing what sounded like an impersonation of Prince Charles. The man whose thoughts I was channelling had a very considered but quite ponderous way of speaking, rather like the Prince.

'If I didn't know any different I'd say there was something almost slightly autistic about this man,' I said as I described the thoughts he was passing on to me. 'But at the same time he has a great way with words and poetry.'

I connected with a lady in the audience. She was slightly sceptical to begin with. So I told her that he was starting to put some particular words into my mouth and I started to quote a poem.

She sat there very quietly at first but I could soon see her eyes glistening. By the time I'd finished the poem she was deeply moved.

'I don't quite know how you did that,' she said. 'That's remarkable, absolutely remarkable.'

She continued, 'My husband wrote poetry. What

115

you are quoting is the last poem he ever wrote and I am the only person who has a copy of it.'

The audience just sat there open-mouthed. I have to admit it was one of those moments where even I was stunned.

The message continued for a brief time after that. He was making highly intellectual jokes that the audience weren't finding funny. But I could tell from his energy—and his wife's laughter—that they were both finding it hilarious.

Afterwards the lady came up to me and thanked me. She said she had seen me on television but that she wasn't overtly interested in mediumship. A friend had persuaded her to come to my demonstration. She'd come along with an inquiring mind and very little expectation. She told me she'd been blown away by what I'd communicated to her.

We chatted for a few minutes during which time I told her how I'd felt in her husband's presence. 'He had this very intense way of thinking about things. I'm sorry to have used the word "autistic" but that was the only way I can describe it, having worked with autistic children in healing situations,' I said.

'That was fine. He was slightly autistic,' she said. 'You described him perfectly and got his way of speaking right too.'

What was so interesting to me about that was the fact that this man had not changed in his essence at all yet. In life this man had been an intellectual. And he had come back from the other side in precisely the same way. In many ways he had offered the same kind of evidence as Raymond had provided his father, Sir Oliver Lodge. His spirit had shown us that while he was no longer a part of his earthly body, his true self remained intact.

Till Death Us Do Part

One aspect of the afterlife that I have began to understand more deeply over the years is the idea of progression. Progression is the process through which the spirits of our loved ones evolve on the other side.

When they first arrive they are very much the same personalities as when they were here on the earthly plane. But as time passes they do evolve emotionally and intellectually, while still retaining the sense of self.

A reading with a lady a few years back was hugely helpful in illustrating how this can work.

The lady wasn't the most pleasant person who has ever sat for me. Far from it, in fact. When she walked into the room for a reading she was abrupt and to the point.

'I hope you can help me with what I have come to find out,' she said, taking off her coat and placing her handbag on the carpet next to the chair I'd offered her.

'I can't promise anything, I'm afraid,' I said, to which she responded with a slightly grumpy shrug of her shoulders.

'Oh dear,' I thought to myself. 'I am going to struggle here.'

Fortunately, however, I quickly sensed that I was in the presence of a man. He didn't exactly seem excited or full of energy. But I felt he had something important that he was burning to communicate through me.

It quickly became clear that he was this lady's husband. It was equally obvious from the outset that they had been in a loveless marriage.

When I brought him through his wife recognised him with a grimace. However, her reaction wasn't quite as bad as that of the lady who, when I brought through her husband a few years earlier, responded with a shooing motion of her hands and said: 'I don't want him. You can send him away. I had no time for him in life and I have certainly not got any time for him now that he's dead.' But, all the same, this lady wasn't exactly overwhelmed by her husband's presence.

It was obvious, however, that he had come through for a reason. It was a couple of years since his passing and he'd clearly evolved.

'He wants you to know that he realises that you shouldn't have behaved that way to each other in life,' I told her. 'He says he knows you never loved him and, to be honest, he felt the same about you.'

He didn't feel any more strongly about her now. What he did feel, however, was a strong desire to wish her happiness in what remained of her earthly life.

'I hope you can find someone who makes you happy in a way I never did,' he said.

As far as I was concerned it was a rather moving message, one that had, I suspected, required a great deal of effort and energy for him to bring through. He wasn't the most eloquent or intelligent of men but he had passed on some thing rather profound.

His wife's reaction was completely cold, however. She simply looked away and mumbled to herself.

118

It was clear that his attempts to be emotionally honest with her had fallen on deaf ears. Unsurprisingly, the reading came to an end soon afterwards.

'Despite what you think of him, he sends his love and best wishes,' I said as his energy faded and I lost the connection.

She wasn't happy that the session had drawn to a close. 'Is that it?' she demanded as she put her coat back on.

As I showed her out of the door she told me that the reason she'd come for a reading was that she was trying to find out what he had done with his money.

'He put it away somewhere where I couldn't get to it,' she grumbled. 'I didn't want all that other nonsense he had for me.'

I made it clear to her that this was a pretty questionable reason to come to a medium in the first place. And I also tried to tell her that his message was actually something she should think about quite deeply.

I might as well have saved my breath, however. She headed off looking as miserable as when she'd arrived.

I found out later that the lady had eventually located her husband's savings thanks to one small detail I'd passed on. But I don't think it improved her happiness one jot.

I had mixed emotions immediately after the reading. Part of me felt sorry for this poor man who had come forward to try to acknowledge their relationship, to accept that he hadn't been a particularly wonderful husband.

But another part of me was satisfied that I had

made such a revealing connection, one that helped me to a greater understanding. I had seen that the man's attempt to reconcile with his wife was actually part of his evolution on the other side. He was becoming a more emotionally developed and intelligent being. I was actually really grateful to have shared the insight he had given me. It was a shame his wife didn't share that view. Maybe some day, somewhere she would ...

An Inconvenient Message

As a medium you have to be very careful about the messages you pass on. Spirits are always brutally honest, sometimes too honest. By directly channelling their communications you can open a real can of worms. As a result, I have learned that there are times when a medium's job is to moderate his messages or keep his mouth firmly shut.

I first learned this early on during my career when I was demonstrating at a Spiritualist church in Crawley. It had been a fairly routine, uneventful demonstration. But then I felt myself in the presence of a grey-haired gentleman.

'I have an elderly man here,' I said. 'He's showing me that he is a grandfather and he is looking to make contact with his granddaughter who is in the audience.'

He gave me a few more details that helped me locate the granddaughter. She was a pretty young girl, probably in her mid to late teens. She was sitting towards the front of the congregation with another, older woman, who I assumed to be her mother.

As the message continued, it was clear that the

young girl had been very close to her grandfather and I could understand why. He had a lovely, gentle aura about him. He told her how much he loved her and how he was often in her presence, watching over her. She was very pleased by his general message, as indeed was I. Until the very end, that is.

The communication was drawing to a close when he showed me one final thought. Looking back on it, I can see that I should have taken a moment to consider it before just repeating it. But I didn't, I simply relayed it to her.

'Oh yes, and your granddad just wants you to know that he's really happy about the forthcoming baby,' I said.

In an instant the atmosphere in the room changed. I'm sure the temperature dropped ten degrees. You could feel the chill running through the air. The young woman's face turned white, as if she'd been drained of all life. In stark contrast to this, the face of the woman sitting with her turned bright red. For a moment the pair were completely oblivious to the other people in the room.

'What's this all about?' the mother asked, turning to her mortified daughter. The daughter sat there mute, unable to speak.

To the embarrassment of myself and everyone else in the church the mother began berating the daughter in front of the entire congregation. 'What have you gone and done? You stupid little girl! I warned you about this. And when were you going to tell me all about it?' she said.

'Maybe you two could sort this out afterwards,' I suggested, trying to restore some semblance of calm to proceedings.

Fortunately, the mother realised that the entire church was looking at them and made an apologetic shrug.

I had, of course, only been doing my job, fulfilling my role as the link between this world and the other one. But at that particular moment I felt like I'd been a complete failure. I also have a job to filter what is being passed along. I hadn't done so in this instance. It was no wonder the girl looked like she could quite happily shoot the messenger.

Afterwards, as they were leaving the church the daughter came up to me and threw me a terrible look. 'Thanks, Colin,' she snapped, looking as if she'd be quite happy to slap me.

After a moment or two, however, she calmed down. 'You were right. I am pregnant. But I'm only fifteen and I haven't told my family yet.'

I felt awful and tried to console her. 'I'm so sorry,' I said. 'If I'd known I wouldn't have passed on that part of the message.'

'It's all right,' she said. 'You've probably helped me. It's forced the situation out into the open.'

It was an important lesson in more ways than one. From the audience's point of view, it illustrated the fact that spirits can come out with uncomfortable truths. People may come along with ideas about what they *want* to hear from their loved ones who have passed over, but the fact is those loved ones may have a very different opinion about what those on this side of life *need* to hear.

From the point of view of a young medium it provided an important lesson. It showed me that sometimes you really had to take care about the information you brought through. Since then, whenever I have sensed information that is particularly sensitive or embarrassing, I generally ask to see the person in private afterwards.

Most of the time it's worked but, inevitably, there are occasions when it doesn't, again because there are occasions when the spirit world insists on presenting things as they really are.

Many years after the Crawley incident I was invited to do a demonstration by a television production company. They were interested in turning my work into a series of programmes. I was invited to go along to a house in Essex where I'd do a reading for a group of strangers. The reading would be filmed with a view to turning it into a pilot for the TV show.

I was quite apprehensive about it. I wasn't sure television was something I wanted to get involved in at that point in my life.

I walked into the house and there were lights and cameras set up. There was also a small gathering of people sitting around in a semi-circle. I could sense immediately that they were a real mixed bag.

I knew that with such a small audience I was unlikely to receive more than one or two messages. So I was conscious of making sure I communicated them as effectively and entertainingly as possible. It was a televised performance after all.

The second message that came through was from a father. He was quite a formidable character, a big man physically. He showed me that he wanted to make contact with his son.

Immediately I was drawn to this guy who was in the room. It turned out he was a policeman, and was very sceptical about what I did. And his father had clearly come to me in order to deliver his son a

123

stinging rebuke.

He began by basically telling him off for not paying enough attention to his teenage son.

'Your father is telling me that he thinks you are always too busy and should be making more time for your son,' I said. 'He knows the dangers of this. That's what he did with you when you were growing up. He is saying: "Don't let history repeat itself. For Christ's sake, do something now while you can still repair your relationship with your son."'

The son seemed unmoved by this and simply sat in his chair with his arms folded, only turning to what I assumed was his wife alongside him to raise his eyebrows mockingly.

His father hadn't finished tearing a strip off his son, however. 'Your father is also saying that you should stop spending so many nights away from home,' I said.

This provoked a bit more of a reaction. The son now started shifting a bit uneasily in his chair, again throwing looks at the woman next to him.

'Your father says, "Start spending more time with your family and sort out your relationship with them,"' I said.

He still sat there in silence, not reacting to what I'd said. The woman too remained stony-faced and speechless.

It was only later that I found out why.

At the end of the demonstration, after the guests had left and the camera crew had packed up their equipment, the producer and I had a chat.

'It went very well, Colin,' he said. 'We got some good stuff but we won't be able to use some of it.'

I was a bit put out by this. 'Why not?' I

demanded to know.

'It was the message from the father to the policeman son,' he said. 'We can't put that out.'

'Why?' I asked again.

'Because the woman there was his mistress, not his wife. If we broadcast them in the audience together and him receiving that message we could get into all sorts of trouble.'

Suddenly it all fell into place. The father was chastising his son for having an affair. No wonder he'd looked so unhappy with what I was telling him.

Once again, I wished I'd kept my mouth closed. The spirit world hadn't been willing, however.

The pilot eventually evolved into my television series *6ixth Sense*, but that particular story never made it on to the screen, for obvious reasons.

SPIRIT SECRET

The Teachings of Silver Birch is a book that has a very special significance for me.

I have spent the last thirty years of my life studying every aspect of mediumship, spiritualism and the spirit world. I have also sought out my own evidence of its existence.

When I was younger, this involved me in soaking up everything I could from other mediums. I went along to demonstrations held by people such as Ursula Roberts and the direct voice medium Leslie Flint. I went to see some outstanding mediums— Stephen O'Brien, Doris Collins and of course Doris Stokes.

I also started to read books like *The*

Teachings of Silver Birch, the wisdom of a very evolved spirit being who had communicated over many years through the editor of *Psychic News*, a highly respected medium called Maurice Barbanell.

Sad to say, much of the 'new age' literature available today is a pale imitation of the articulate and intelligent teachings that emerged thanks to people such as Maurice Barbanell.

Silver Birch's teachings are regarded as some of the most important ever communicated. He talked of how the spirit world has a hierarchy that works together to enable communication. He described how spirits had to 'lower their vibration' in order to communicate with the earthly plane. He also passed on a huge body of wise sayings and teachings.

As I absorbed the extent of the wisdom that had been accumulated through the centuries-old history of spiritualism and mediumship, I began to see that the spirit world was the repository of a vast amount of knowledge.

Love Me, Love My Dog

No one passes over without leaving something behind to remind their loved ones of their time on this earthly plane. The most obvious legacy, of course, is our children and grandchildren, brothers and sisters and other relatives. They, quite literally, represent our living flesh and blood.

Others leave a different mark behind. Some, for

instance, live on in examples of their work, whether it's written words or works of art, or physical things they have built during their lifetimes. But we also leave behind subtler things that continue to live on after our passing.

In dealing with the loss of a loved one, people often lose sight of this; they fail to appreciate that the person who has passed over remains here in some sense. And in doing so they erect a kind of barrier that can make it harder for them to deal with their loss.

A good example of this was that of a lady I met at a social gathering in Sussex a few years ago. She was an elegant lady, in her early sixties, who had lost her husband a couple of years earlier. She had made huge strides in getting on with her life. She hadn't made the mistake so many widows and widowers make of hiding behind her curtains and cutting herself off from the world. She was very active socially. Nevertheless there was still a slight sadness to her and so I wasn't surprised in the least when towards the end of our chat at this social gathering she asked me for a private reading. She had been lovely, convivial company during the party so, even though I was fully booked for more than a year ahead, I agreed.

A few weeks later she turned up at my home.

When the reading got under way it didn't take long to connect with her husband. It was one of those instances where, I felt, he had been waiting for an opportunity to connect with her. He seemed a very decent, warm and loving man who had clearly thought the world of his wife. He also seemed to have a deep affection for something else as well.

'Your husband is showing me that he loved two things in life,' I said as the connection strengthened.

When I said this she smiled. 'Yes, I can understand that, Colin,' she nodded.

As she said this my mind was filled with an image of a large dog, running around a field. I also saw him and his wife walking hand in hand behind the dog.

'He is showing me that he loved you and he loved his dog,' I said.

Again, she smiled. 'That's him, you've got my husband,' she said.

It was a strong connection and the husband was very keen to keep communicating to his wife.

'He's showing me that when he was alive the dog wouldn't have anything to do with you,' I said.

She nodded.

'In fact you and the dog hated each other,' I said.

'Yes, that's right,' she agreed, grimacing slightly.

'Does the name Buster mean anything?' I asked.

'That's the dog's name,' she confirmed.

I then saw another image of the dog running around. This time, however, I saw his wife alone in the field.

'Your husband is showing me that since he's passed over your relationship with Buster has changed. It used to be that Buster wouldn't come anywhere near you or sit with you—he even used to growl at you,' I said.

'Yes.'

'But things began to alter between you almost as soon as your husband passed over.'

This brought a tear to her eye. 'That's so true,

128

Colin,' she sighed. 'Do you know, the dog and I started to get on from the day he died. It was almost as if we were there to console each other.

'My husband was in hospital and he died there. On the day he died I was getting ready to drive over to the hospital to see him. All of a sudden the dog started howling. Five minutes later I got a phone call from the hospital to say that he had died,' she said. 'Me and the dog are best friends now.'

She had always taken it as a sign from her husband that Buster had been there to care for her. But she hadn't really thought of Buster representing something of her husband living on. It had taken the spirit world to show her the truth of the situation.

8.

HOW THE SPIRITS CAN COMFORT YOU

'It is only when the soul is in adversity that some of its greatest possibilities can be realised.' SILVER BIRCH

By far the most common kind of communication I give people are messages of confirmation. Anyone who has been to one of my demonstrations will have seen them: a loved one or friend may come through purely to let those they have left behind know that they have made it safely to the other side. Alternatively a husband or wife or child may communicate with me in order to confirm one crucial piece of information that their loved ones have desperately been waiting to hear.

Often these messages are a huge release for the recipient. The comfort, reassurance and information they provide helps them get on with the rest of their own earthly life.

The spirit world is a place of infinite complexity and mystery, so it is never easy to predict how, when or through whom these confirmations will materialise. It's perhaps not surprising then that during the course of my career, I've witnessed the spirit world deliver all sorts of strange, unexpected and extremely emotional messages of this kind.

The Lost Soldier

During the period when I was a trance medium, I

was always glad to welcome sceptics to my séances. On more than one occasion they arrived full of doubts and left with their view of this world—and the one beyond it—changed for ever.

One such man joined a séance I was asked to conduct in Bristol a number of years ago. He was in his late sixties or early seventies and was a guest of one of the organisers. He admitted beforehand that he doubted very much that what I did was genuine. He was a science teacher and a very logical man. He was confident that he wouldn't be surprised or convinced by what he experienced.

'I respect your right to do what you do but I don't believe in it,' he said, politely. 'I'll be interested to see what happens though.'

As usual I was in a trance state so had the events related to me afterwards by members of the circle who were there.

It had begun with a man coming through to me. He was a soldier and he had been dead many years. He was also an evolved spirit, at peace with himself and his existence. The traumas he had suffered during wartime seemed to have been consigned to the past.

His energy was being focused on another man who was in the room.

'My name is William and I came from a large family here in the West Country. I want to make contact with my brother, who is here.'

He identified the science teacher with whom I'd spoken before the séance. When I made this apparent he looked quizzically at me, apparently.

'I had a brother named William, but . . .' he said, his voice trailing off. 'I also have three brothers, John, Edward and Terence.'

At that William's body language changed dramatically. 'Yes, that's right,' he said.

William went on to describe being involved in the Allied invasion of northern France during the Normandy landings towards the end of the Second World War. He described in vivid detail how he had been part of an advancing battalion which had come under fire from German aeroplanes.

He had been hit and had fallen into an open ditch. Unable to clamber his way out, he had lain there for a day before giving up on his fight for life. He had died there and had never been found.

This was 50 years after he'd gone missing.

What was so fascinating about it was that the soldier hadn't just talked about himself. He'd mentioned another brother, Edward, who had been in the RAF. He had been shot down and—again—hadn't been found.

Now, given the level of scepticism the teacher had displayed, I'm not sure whether this evidence on its own would have been enough to persuade him that I really was communicating with his long-lost brother, who was speaking through me in what resembled his earthly voice.

What happened next, however, left him in no doubt.

The way it was described to me afterwards was that William's brother suddenly stood up and gestured as if he was wrapping his arms around someone. Apparently, as he did so he had tears rolling down his face.

'Do you know what became of Edward?' the brother then asked.

'He is with me. He couldn't make it here tonight,' William said. 'But he is here and has been for a long time.'

It was a very emotional moment for the man; one that, I'm sure, he hadn't expected in a million years. He openly admitted afterwards that he'd had all his preconceptions shattered.

'I'm overwhelmed,' he told me when the circle had broken and he had come over to thank me.

As we chatted along with some other members of the group he revealed that his brother's fate had long been a mystery within his family. 'None of us has never known what happened to William. He was declared missing in action but we were never able to find out where he was last seen or what happened to him,' he said.

'It wasn't even as if we could go to one of the sites with a mass grave. We had no idea where he died. For my parents in particular it was very difficult to deal with not knowing how he met his death.'

One of the circle members had described to me how he had stood up during the séance.

I was curious about this.

'Why did you stand up?' I asked him.

'Because I saw him. I saw William. He partially materialised in front of me,' he said.

He was still very emotional about it, I could tell.

'I could feel him holding me and I wanted to feel him back. I couldn't feel him but it was enough that I felt him holding me.'

As he came to terms with what had happened he had a little chuckle to himself at one point.

'When I go back to school and tell them what happened they are going to think I'm mad, absolutely off my rocker,' he laughed. 'But no one is going to persuade me that it didn't happen. I know what I experienced tonight and I know I will never forget it.'

A Voice From The Past

There have been times when I too have found myself wanting to receive confirmation of some detail or other. Fortunately, the spirits have always been helpful.

For instance, my guide, Magnus, was always very secretive about his real identity. I didn't doubt that he had lived, but a part of me always wanted some evidence, some proof that he had done the things that he said he'd done, been to the places he said he'd been to.

Some people had suggested that I looked into his family tree. I didn't want to do that. If he didn't want to tell me the full details of his life then that was his right. But I did yearn for some evidence, some little clue about his time on this earthly plane. And the spirit world came up trumps as usual.

One day I travelled down to a Spiritual Hall in Portsmouth to do a trance demonstration. Just before the demonstration was about to start this very, very elderly lady walked into the room and headed for a seat in the front row. I couldn't help noticing her. She was so old, close to about one hundred, I'd have guessed.

It turned out she wasn't familiar to me, she was familiar to Magnus. When I went off into trance and Magnus came through as usual, he immediately began to speak to her.

Talking to those present afterwards it was clear from the conversation that Magnus had known this

134

lady's grandfather. He had spoken about the fact that her family had a mill somewhere in the English countryside. As a young man he had visited her family home often. He told the lady how he would go and see her family twice a year.

She had responded to what he said, apparently.

At one point Magnus said that he remembered the lady when she was little girl.

'Your voice hasn't changed at all,' she told him. 'I can even remember your full name,' she said rather tantalisingly.

'And yes, that will remain a secret between you and me,' he had said. Magnus has always been very cagey about his real name.

Afterwards I had a chat with the lady. Rather annoyingly she was as cagey as Magnus. 'I'm under orders as to what I can tell you but I do remember your guide very well,' she said.

I was fascinated. 'Tell me more,' I said.

'Well, when I was a little girl he was a friend of my grandfather's. He was quite a stern man. I can't say I was ever very fond of him; I was quite frightened by him, truth be told,' she said.

As it happened, only a few weeks before that Magnus had been talking in my regular circle about his children. He had spoken about his eldest son, Valentine.

So I asked the lady whether she remembered his children's names.

'His eldest son was called Valentine,' she said.

That's when I knew she really had known him. I don't know whether it was Magnus or someone else in the spirit world who arranged for the meeting to take place. Whoever it was, I was delighted they had taken the trouble.

135

Roland

The spirit world is subtle and resourceful. It doesn't always have to show itself in the form of physical manifestations of spirits or dramatic messages. It can show itself in much more mundane and down-to-earth ways, and the most common way it manifests itself is through signs.

I experience all sorts of signs all the time. One of the most memorable—and amusing—I've had in recent years came from a good friend called Roland.

We'd been close friends since I was a young man. Roland was a very warm and fun-loving character, one of those friends who had that precious ability to cheer me up whenever I saw him. We all need a friend like that.

But then in his early forties, Roland developed cancer of the oesophagus. It was devastating, given that he didn't smoke, had a good diet and drank very moderately. Witnessing Roland's decline was hard. When he'd been well he had been a well-filled-out man but as he fought his cancer he shrank to skeletal form. It was tragic to see.

Just before he passed over I went to see him. We'd spoken openly about the fact that he was going to die. I asked him if he'd made arrangements for the funeral and afterwards.

He wasn't religious but he told me he'd made arrangements for a minister to oversee the ceremony and was going to have music by Dusty Springfield. He was also going to have Edith Piaf singing *'Je Ne Regrette Rien'*. Then he told me he was going to have everyone sing 'All Things Bright and Beautiful'.

'Why are you having that?' I asked.

Roland was gay and had a very impish sense of humour. He was having the music played for his own amusement, he told me. 'If there is an afterlife,' he said, 'I want to be able to see all the queens at the back of the church singing "All Things Bright and Beautiful" while waving their daffodils.'

When he finally succumbed to his cancer, the arrangements were made for his funeral in accordance with his wishes. My mother went along with me to the service because she had been very friendly with Roland. We sat in the front row next to his brother.

I'd told my mother about what Roland had chosen for his music. When it got to the point where the minister introduced the hymn, my mum gave me a nudge and smile.

I turned round and there was this selection of his gay friends, holding flowers and doing just as he had imagined. I really admired him for that. He was a man who wanted to create a joke at his funeral. He wanted it to be seen that even in the afterlife he was funny.

In the days and weeks following Roland's passing, I'd expected to get a message of some kind. Most of my friends and family have usually connected to me quite quickly when they've passed over. But he didn't.

In fact it took him a good fifteen years to get through to me. And, typically of Roland, he did it in a way that made me smile.

I was on the phone one day talking to a medium friend of mine.

'Oh, Colin,' she said at one point, 'I meant to

tell you that I have just bought an electric organ. It's wonderful—it's called a Roland organ.'

Before I could respond she said, 'That's funny, as soon as I said that I got a man standing alongside me. He's standing here now and is saying, "Roland, that's my name."'

I didn't say anything, I just waited to hear if there was any more. I guessed it was the Roland I knew.

'He's just told me he is a friend of yours,' and then she described his cancer condition and related a personal experience that we had had together in Bournemouth.

This rang very true immediately. Years earlier Roland and I had gone to Bournemouth on holiday.

She then produced even more evidence, which left me in absolutely no doubt that she had him with her.

The funny thing about that was that the first thing I thought of when she mentioned she had Roland with her was his funeral. Immediately I'd remembered how he'd managed to put a smile on my face, something that he'd been able to do in life too.

I could have remembered the awful tragedy of the cancer that had killed him. But I hadn't. Instead I'd remembered something that reflected his whole life rather than the brief and painful period at its end.

That is the beauty of the spirit world. It connects you to the truth, the essence of those who have passed over. I remembered the real Roland, the man with a great sense of humour who had been my friend.

138

The Little Blackbird

Messages can be the simplest and most profound communications.

Quite recently, I was demonstrating at a theatre in Ireland and was connecting through a gentleman. He had a message for his family, but he also had a message for someone else in the auditorium.

It took a while to locate the lady in question.

'He says it won't mean anything to anyone but you, but your husband says that the little blackbird in the garden was down to him.'

The impact this had on the lady was absolutely wonderful. Immediately her face was wreathed in a broad smile.

'Obviously you understand that,' I said to her.

'Yes, I do,' she said.

I didn't press her further on it. I didn't need to. The message couldn't have been more well received. After the show, however, she came up to me and explained.

'When he was alive he would always say that, when he passed over—which he knew he would before me, as he was older and less healthy than me—he would give me a sign that he was safely on the other side,' she said.

She continued, 'We have a water fountain in the garden. He said he'd come back as a little blackbird and sit there one day. I saw a little blackbird there a couple of weeks ago and came along tonight in the hope that he might confirm it was him. He did.'

As I say, sometimes the simplest messages are often the most profound. That was certainly the case here.

Silver Bells For Christmas

One of the most important messages I ever passed on from the spirit world was to another medium. It is no exaggeration to say it changed my life.

Leslie Flint was, quite rightly, regarded as the finest physical medium of the twentieth century in this country. Born in 1911, he had grown up in London and had begun communicating with the spirit world at the age of eight. Before the First World War he had gone on to become the most celebrated medium of his time. Most notably he had used his amazing gift for voice-mediumship to bring through messages from people ranging from an East End boy called Micky, who had died in an accident in Camden Town in 1910, to famous people from the actor Rudolph Valentino to Noel Coward and even Queen Victoria. Following his communication with the latter, the Queen's daughter, Princess Louise, invited Leslie to give her a private reading.

When I was developing as a medium, I was fortunate enough to be invited along to a couple of his circles. Whilst there I had received amazing communications from my grandfather Laurie.

I'd never actually spoken to Leslie in person. His séances were very formal, rigidly run affairs. The guests would arrive and be ushered into the reading room. Once everyone was ready, Leslie would come, speaking to no one, and the séance would take place.

At the end of the circle he would leave again without speaking to those in the circle. You would then be escorted from the house, told 'thank you very much' and off you went. It was the way he'd operated for many years and I had no problems with it at all.

Leslie used to have a close companion, Bram, with whom he shared his life at his home by the sea in Hove. When Leslie was in his late seventies, and in poor health himself, Bram died suddenly, leaving Leslie devastated.

About a year or so after Bram's death I began doing trance demonstrations in a psychic bookshop in Brighton. Initially it was for thirty or forty people but it soon became so popular that we had to hire a hall to accommodate the 250 or 300 people turning up from all over the country.

At one of the last demonstrations at the bookshop we crammed eighty people into the crowded space. My spirit guide Magnus was speaking and answering questions from people in the audience.

Suddenly he stopped and said: 'I don't do this very often but I am going to stand aside and let another gentleman come through who wants to speak to someone in the audience.' He stood aside.

Apparently, this voice came through and addressed a man who was sitting in the audience. The voice simply said, 'Oh hello, lovey.'

The man was very cautious. 'I think I know who you are but can you confirm it, please?' he said.

'You should know me after all these years,' said the voice.

The two men had started talking about photography, which was a shared interest apparently.

Clearly the man in the audience was satisfied with the identity of the spirit communicating through me.

'Do you have a message for our mutual friend?' he asked at one point.

'Yes. Please tell Daddy that there will be silver bells for Christmas.'

And with that, apparently, he just went, handing back to Magnus.

When I'm in trance I'm totally oblivious to what's going on. So when it was all over and the woman organising the evening came over to me I asked her how it had gone.

'It was quite unusual,' she said. 'Magnus stopped talking to let someone else speak.'

'Oh, who was it?' I asked, surprised.

'I don't know. It was a private conversation between these two gentlemen.'

I thought nothing more about it until, about three weeks later, I got a phone call from Carol Hawkins whom I had grown to know after her close friend Kenneth Williams had come through at one of our regular circles.

'Colin, Leslie Flint would like to meet you,' she said.

'Really?' I asked, taken aback. It was as if I'd been asked to go and see my hero. 'Why?'

'He wants you to do a séance for him.'

Now I was really shocked. 'He wants me to do a séance for him?'

'Yes,' she said. 'And a selected group of his friends.'

I said I'd have to bring a member of my circle with me because I didn't do these things alone.

'That will probably be fine,' she said. Sure enough she called me back later, having checked with Leslie, to say that I could bring my circle members too.

So the appointed day arrived and we went along.

I was very nervous. I was being asked to do a séance for the master.

When we went in there was a group of his friends waiting. They were friendly enough; they all thanked me for coming along but they were being cagey. They weren't saying much to me.

After a while we all went into Leslie's séance room. Then this old man was brought into the room. It had been a good couple of years since I'd seen Leslie and it took me a while to realise it was him. It was obvious that he had been so devastated by the loss of Bram that all his energy had gone. He really seemed a pale shadow of his former self.

I immediately began having doubts about what I was doing. A voice in my head starting saying, 'This is a mistake, you shouldn't be doing this, he isn't well enough for this.' But his friends seemed keen for us to continue, the séance was ready to begin and I couldn't really back out.

So, as usual, I went into a trance. I never have any concept of time when I am in this state. When I come out it seems as if I have nodded off for a second or two, yet an hour or more can have passed.

As I came out this evening the atmosphere in the room had been completely transformed. It had been rather heavy and grim-faced before I'd gone into the trance. Now everyone was smiling and seemed extremely excited. No one was more excited than Leslie, who looked completely different, as if he'd been born again. He was full of energy and grabbed my arm.

'Come with me, young man,' he said. He rushed me downstairs to his study and sat me down. 'I have to tell you what happened,' he smiled. 'Bram just came through to speak to me through you.'

I was pleased.

'But I knew he wanted to speak to me through you any way because he's communicated through you once already.'

I didn't know what he was talking about.

'I'm sorry, Mr Flint, I don't know where you got that from but I think you are mistaken,' I said.

He just shook his head. 'No, no, no, you have— listen to this,' he said.

He then produced a tape which he played. There was this voice speaking through me. It had been recorded in the bookshop in Brighton by the man I'd communicated with in the audience. It turned out he was a friend of both Bram and Leslie.

I didn't even know that these people were there, let alone who they were or that they were taping the demonstration.

'That's Bram,' he said. 'The day of the demonstration that you did I had been talking to a group of friends. Bram and I had a set of antique Christmas bells and I'd said I wasn't going to put them up this year because I didn't have the heart for it.'

Leslie also told me that Daddy was Bram's nickname for him because he was twenty years older than him.

After that I did two other séances for Leslie before he passed away. He also wrote, totally unnecessarily, to *Psychic News* afterwards. He said that, although there had been many mediums who had claimed to have got a message from Bram, through my trance and physical mediumship I had given him irrevocable evidence of Bram's survival.

It was a huge moment for me. I think it was the turning point in my life if I'm honest.

My career had been doing quite well before this. I was gaining in popularity and more people were coming to see me. But there was a barrier I was coming up against time and again. The Spiritualist community is quite hierarchical and when you are a young medium you are often told 'you're quite good but you're just a boy'.

The reading I did for Leslie marked the moment I turned from a boy into a man. In my own mind I was no longer the youngster who had to look up to these older mediums. I felt like their equal now.

Some of the older mediums, who shall remain unnamed, were quite cruel and spiteful when I was younger. When I reached this point in popularity they became much warmer and friendlier towards me. I think I changed too.

In the wake of the reading I re-read Leslie's wonderful book *Voices In The Dark* and read the interviews he did with a friend of mine, George Cranley.

Leslie defined what it is to be a medium as well as anyone has ever done. Our purpose, he said, is 'to help humanity, to give comfort from the point of view that death is not the end, that the person they've known and loved still exists and at times is able to come near them, and that one day they will meet again on the Other Side of life.'

And in doing that, he added: 'We have to realise

145

that we had a great responsibility placed on our shoulders. We have to treat mediumship with respect and we have to do it in the best possible way we can, to give people the realisation that we are genuinely, sincerely anxious to uplift and comfort them. I believe we must present this in a way that will command respect.'

I have tried to live up to that.

Where's Your Mamma Gone?

The spirit world communicates with me in a number of ways, mostly in the form of vibrations of thoughts. But sometimes it is the vibration of sounds that comes through.

It can be a very unusual way of communicating a message. It can also be quite a powerful one, as a memorable message I gave to a lady during a show in the northwest of England once illustrated.

It was the first message of the evening and came through almost as soon as I brought up the house lights to look at the audience.

I'd been aware of a female presence ever since arriving at the theatre that evening. She had died quite young and left behind two young children. I connected with a lady in the audience who confirmed that she had been eleven when her mother Nancy had passed over, while her brother was even younger. I was aware of a great deal of sound during the communication, in particular I kept hearing sirens. I couldn't decide whether they were an ambulance or a fire engine.

'Do you understand something to do with a fire engine or an ambulance?' I said to her.

'Yes,' she nodded. 'Both. There was a fire in her

146

house shortly before she died and soon after that she had been rushed to hospital in an ambulance.'

Confident now that I had connected with the right person in the audience, I felt the communication intensify. Soon the ringing of sirens and bells was replaced by a very different sound.

I recognised it immediately and couldn't help laughing at what I was hearing.

'I'm listening to a song I haven't heard for years,' I said. ' "Chirpy Chirpy Cheep Cheep" by Middle of the Road. Do you understand that?'

The lady nodded.

'It seems to have some special significance,' I said.

'Yes, it does,' she agreed. 'Just as my mother died, that song came on, on the radio.' She was a little upset at the memory and took a moment to compose herself.

'Because of that I couldn't listen to it for years and years,' she went on. She said that the chorus, 'Where's your mamma gone . . . far, far away', had been too much for her to take.

At that point, however, a broad smile started spreading across her face. 'But now I sing it in karaoke!'

I had a feeling that there was some deeper purpose to this message. The daughter had clearly moved on in her life and had come to terms with her mother's passing.

As the communication resumed, Nancy showed me two men, her husband and her son, the brother of the lady in the audience. As she did so, I began to feel a real sense of anger within her. She still felt angry at the way she'd had to leave her young children behind and her husband grieving terribly.

'I am seeing that your father was terribly emotionally scarred by her passing,' I said.

'Yes, he was,' the daughter nodded.

'That pain went on for four years.'

'No, only two years. He passed away two years after her,' she said, shaking her head now.

'No, I'm sorry, it went on for four years. For the equivalent of two years on this side of life, they were kept apart on the other side.'

I could sense, however, that while the daughter had moved on, her brother hadn't. 'It took him longer.'

'It did,' she said.

By bringing through the song, however, Nancy's spirit had shown how life did go on. According to the lyrics of that song, their mother had gone 'far, far away'. But as her musical evidence had revealed, she hadn't really.

If only they'd been able to realise that sooner.

Ghosts

Mediumship is a form of communication. And because it is a form of communication, it works better at some times than others. There are times when messages don't sink in immediately. There are times when they get garbled or misinterpreted. The end result of all this is that it can sometimes take a while for the spirits to get over what they are trying to say.

This is why I don't actually mind if during a public performance someone says, 'Oh I didn't understand that.' I have long since given up worrying about what the sceptics or doubters in the audience think. It doesn't bother me if they leave there thinking, 'Oh he didn't get that right.' I have faith in the spirit world and I have learned to trust it more than the earthly world in instances like this.

Experience has taught me to ask people to mull over what I have told them. Often it's only afterwards, when they digest what has happened, that they feel the impact. Sometimes I also suggest that people go home and check details. When they do they are often shocked at what they discover.

So it was with the mother of a little boy who came through to me when I was performing at a charity show in Blackpool.

She had come along, as so many people do, looking for some kind of comfort after the loss of her son, Brett. He had been only seven years old when he'd died less than a year previously. The loss was still very raw for her.

The spirit of a young boy came through to me. I felt it was this lady's son. But even though the mother was desperate for evidence that it was him, it was difficult to find a detail that proved beyond doubt that it was.

It wasn't because of what he was telling me, I hasten to say. He was a very communicative little boy. It was more that, like any parent, the mother didn't know absolutely every detail there was to know about him.

As the reading went on, I told her that her son was telling me that he used to draw pictures of ghosts. He told me he was fascinated by them.

'No, he didn't,' the mother said, almost dismissively. 'I never saw him drawing ghosts.'

I knew what I was being shown by the boy. 'Yes,

he did. You've got a stack of his old drawings and colouring books stored away at home, haven't you?'

'Yes,' she said.

'Have you never wondered what those strange blobby shapes are that he used to put in every corner of his drawings?' I asked.

She just looked at me bemused. 'Sorry, Colin, I really don't know what you mean.'

'Don't worry if you don't understand it now,' I said. 'I am sure this is what he is telling me, so tomorrow morning when you are at home have a look at those books and you will see what I mean.'

She nodded and said she would.

I didn't really expect to hear back from her, but within twenty-four hours I'd got a message from her via my page on Facebook. Many people communicate with me in this way, and where possible I try to reply.

'Colin, I had to get in contact with you. I went to look at the drawing and colouring books and I'm really sorry to have doubted you. You were absolutely right. There are those blobby drawings in every single corner. He has drawn pictures of ghosts on every page.'

I was relieved. I had sensed that Brett had been trying to stimulate his family's healing process by coming through to me the previous day. In order to do it convincingly he knew he had to come up with a really telling detail. It had taken a while but in the end he had succeeded.

I was delighted for both him and his mother that the communication had finally made sense. For his mother, in particular, it must have been an enormous relief and comfort.

'Death—the last sleep? No, it is the final awakening.' WALTER SCOTT

My Darling Dear

When I first started to develop a name as a trance and physical medium a lot of people would write requesting to come to our séances. I'd never know exactly who was going to be there on any one night. I'd just turn up on a Tuesday at the flat in Hove where the circle always gathered and we'd have a guest.

One evening a lady and a gentleman were there. Another lady came through in spirit and identified herself as Margaret, the man's first wife. The husband became very emotional, as was the lady sitting next to him, his second wife. She had been Margaret's best friend.

It transpired Margaret had been extremely unwell, but before she had passed over she had made her husband promise that he wouldn't marry again. However, as much as he'd loved her, he and the best friend had in their joint grief fallen in love. They had eventually married.

They both felt terribly guilty but now Margaret told them that her attitude had changed since she'd passed over. She said she was glad that they had one another.

Just as the séance was coming to an end she asked the husband, 'Darling, would you like me to sing to you?'

'Oh, that would be lovely,' he said.

Apparently this lady had the most amazing soprano voice. In this amazing voice she sang

Evelyn Laye's 'My Dearest Dear'. This was in physical séance conditions.

The husband said afterwards that it had been her voice and that she had sung him their favourite song, which he had had played at the funeral. For him everything else had been evidence. But that was the icing on the cake.

I was told later that the man and his wife had held each other throughout the séance, just crying.

I had a chat with them afterwards in the kitchen. 'Young man,' he said, 'I am a magistrate. It's my job to assess evidence. And if anyone ever asks me I will vouch for you and your gift. Because what was produced tonight through your mediumship was for me undeniable evidence of my first wife's survival.'

The Copper Pans

'If you knock on a door and it does not open, do not push. If you push the door gently and it opens, that is for you. You cannot go through a closed door. Too many people in your world waste time and effort banging at closed doors.' SILVER BIRCH

Some people have to wait many years to get a message from the other side. Others receive communications frequently. What makes the difference? Why do some people seem to have a direct line to the afterlife while others do not?

Well, there are a lot of factors, but one thing I have noticed over the years is that the people who seem to get the most consistent communication are those who have developed a very positive attitude towards friends and loved ones who have passed over. They don't necessarily become spiritualists. Many have no religious convictions, or they stick to their own faith. But they do have this very forward-looking, optimistic outlook and a very particular way of thinking about those who have passed over.

People are all different, of course, so this attitude can show itself in different ways. Sometimes, for instance, people are able to imagine and visualise their loved ones living this very full, pain-free existence on the other side of life. Often they are also individuals who are very relaxed about whether or not they are going to receive a message. Typically they come along to me and say: 'Yes, it would be lovely if you came through with a message from this person but if you don't that's OK as well because I know they are OK on the other side.'

What's also very significant is that these people seem to be delighted for other people when they get messages. They spread the word about the power of mediumship and its ability to bring hope, joy, comfort and understanding into people's lives.

No one exemplified all these qualities better than a lady called Kathy for whom I used to read on a regular basis for many years. She was an absolutely committed spiritualist, as had been her husband who had passed over a number of years before I first met her.

She had been sad at her husband's passing, naturally. But she had always had a truly positive and mature attitude about it. She knew he had gone over to the spirit world and she knew he was safe and at peace there. She also knew she would join him there in due course. So in the meantime she got on with her life and tried to make contact with him as often as she could.

When I first met her she told me she'd seen a number of mediums over the years. I was fascinated. They were people who won't mean much to the wider world but within the spiritualist medium movement they were big names—people like Gordon Higginson, Ronald Strong, Estelle Roberts and Bill Redman, as well as a remarkable young medium Mark Stevens, who passed over tragically at a very young age.

For about ten years I was her choice of medium for an annual sitting. I used to sit for her once a year, on her birthday. It used to be her treat, although it was as much of a treat for me as it was for her. Sometimes I would go over to her little bungalow in Hassocks and have tea with her.

I used to put a complete afternoon to one side when she was coming for a reading because we would talk for hours afterwards. When I read for her it was usually her husband or her parents who would come through. What amazed me in the ten years that I read for her was that the information was never the same. It was always about different events in their time together, different observations about what they were doing with their lives. She was always so happy when they came through.

One day she said something that I felt was very significant. 'To be honest, Colin, these messages are just a little bonus,' she said to me. 'I don't have these sittings because I need them. I feel them with me all the time. I talk to my husband and my mum and dad every day. But it's just nice to hear them through you.'

I thought this was a fantastic attitude.

Kathy told me how she also drew on the spirits for advice. 'If I'm ever having a bad day, I only have to sit down and think of one of them and what their advice would be. I always seem to be able to sort my problems out by thinking what they would do in this situation,' she confided.

She was not a medium herself, although she did do some work as a healer. She had simply developed this really positive attitude to her loved ones, which meant that she was always able to feel their influence.

There was something else that, I think, helped her. I often find that people who are uptight or overly desperate to receive a message come away from readings or demonstrations disappointed. On the other hand, those who come along with a light, relaxed attitude seem to receive communications.

Kathy was a perfect example of this. She always came across as being like a little girl. Everything was exciting to her. She used to talk nineteen to the dozen.

She also had this absolute joy in spreading the word about spiritualism and mediumship. She never hesitated to tell people about what she did and was completely unapologetic about it.

'I don't care if people think I'm a batty old woman, I know what I have experienced in my life and I just wish them half the joy that it's brought me,' she told me once.

Yet she was also someone who didn't take the spirit world and its messages for granted. She could still be immensely moved by the communications she received.

I remember one very lovely reading she had with me. It actually did make her cry.

Her mother came through. She had died when Kathy was extremely young so Kathy had no living memory of her. She had been raised by her dad, to whom she was extremely close.

Kathy's mother described how the family had a lovely set of copper saucepans. To please her dad one day Kathy had cleaned all the pans, but she had made a right mess of it and had got really upset.

She had also got herself into a real panic. He tended to get home at the same time every evening. As the clock ticked down to the time when he came through the door Kathy was getting into more and more of a state. She thought her dad would come home before she'd finished and she was afraid he would be cross because of the mess she'd made.

During the message her mother talked about how during the last fifteen minutes before her dad arrived home Kathy had somehow managed to get everything cleared up.

'You smiled to yourself afterwards and said, "I don't know how I managed that!" ' I said.

I went on, 'Your mother is telling me that even though you couldn't see her and you couldn't hear her, she was helping you get the copper saucepans sorted out before your dad came home.'

Kathy was in floods of tears at this, but they were happy tears.

She was an amazing lady. In the years that I knew her she was one of those people in my life who taught me most about being spiritual and what being spiritual means.

She came not because she needed to. She didn't come to strengthen her belief because you couldn't have done that, you couldn't have made it more strong. She accepted absolutely. She used to come to sittings because she liked to go away and tell not just friends and family but also total strangers about what she'd experienced.

It wasn't a question of forcing it. She simply told people and wished that they had the same experiences.

Sister Act

I think all mediums have a huge responsibility. Our job is not just about being a message telegraph service. We have this equal responsibility to train and prepare audiences to be receptive to communication. This may sound a little harsh—and I don't mean it to be—but people have to realise that when there is a demonstration going on they are all circuits in a machine and if they are not prepared to play their part to make it happen then they have no right to go home whingeing about the fact that they didn't get a message.

It's not always easy, of course. Sometimes I'll walk out on to the stage, look at the audience and think I'm going to have to work on them first before I can even begin to start communicating and bringing messages through. I have to tell them that they can't all sit there with their arms crossed and expressions on their faces that are saying, 'Come on then, Mr Clever, prove it.'

I have to explain to these people that they are shutting the door not just in my face but on all their friends, all the family and all the loved ones who are on the other side as well. They've got to open up and be prepared to be a part of the occasion.

I have found that there are certain venues—the Manchester Opera House, the Alexandra in Birmingham, the Princess Theatre in Torquay, the Edinburgh Playhouse and the Theatre Royal Brighton spring immediately to mind—where for some reason whenever I have worked there the audiences have all seemed to be playing their part.

Another venue with a great, communal atmosphere that seems to be extremely conducive to demonstrations of mediumship is the Fairfield Halls in Croydon, south London. I have staged demonstrations there several times over the years and the atmosphere can be electric.

I never worry about the number of messages I get across. I am in the business of quality, not quantity. But on some occasions, for whatever reason, quality and quantity come together and I bring through the most remarkable series of communications. That's the way it was on one particular night at the Fairfield Halls. The audience there got it—they had really got it into their heads that they were going to get something out of the evening by watching other people receiving messages.

One of them will always stick in my mind.

Halfway through the show that night I felt myself in the presence of a young woman. 'I have got a young lady here who is trying to connect to her sister. You are not twins but you looked very much alike,' I said.

'And she is showing me a lovely image of you as

teenagers standing in front of a mirror, holding hairbrushes as you sing along to Barbra Streisand and Donna Summer's version of "Enough Is Enough".'

Specific details like that usually produce a swift response in the audience and sure enough a young woman put her hand up. It's a very big venue, the Fairfield Halls, so it was hard to see her. She was sitting in the stalls towards the back of the theatre.

'Is this understandable to you, my love?' I asked her.

'Yes, Colin,' she said.

As the message continued it became clear the sister had passed over years earlier in tragic circumstances, dying of cancer in what seemed to be her teens or thereabouts. She showed me images of her and her sister talking a lot, sharing a lot of laughter and a lot of tears too.

During the message, I had no inkling of what the two sisters had done for a living. But I got a very strong feeling that the death of one sister had effectively ended her sister's career as well. She'd tried to carry on without her but her career had fizzled out.

'That's right, I suppose,' the lady confirmed. 'We were a double act really and without her it wasn't an act any more.'

The circumstances had, apparently, been very difficult for the sister who had been left here on this earthly plane. Her sister said she'd been watching over her as she'd picked up the pieces of her life and got on with things in a dignified way.

The funny thing about the message was that, beyond the image of them singing as children, there were no references to music or dancing or

159

the pop industry. It was a much more down-to-earth, human message, about how much this one sister missed the other sister.

As the message drew to an end and the spirit of the sister began to fade, she left her sibling with the thought that she was extremely proud of the way she'd conducted her life since her untimely passing.

'I was always proud you were my sister and I still am,' she said.

Her sister was so far back in the audience that I couldn't see her. But as the message finished I was aware that a lot of people seemed to be peering over to get a closer look at the lady. A lot of others seemed to be very emotional too.

It was a genuinely moving message, the kind that often brings a tear to people's eyes because it is so universal. So I didn't really think anything more of it. It was only as we came off stage for the intermission that one of the crew came up to me.

'Do you know who that was?' he asked.

'No,' I said. 'I could barely see her.'

When he told me I recognised the name immediately. She had been one half of a pop act that the two sisters had formed together in the 1980s. At the time they had been very successful, producing a string of top ten hits.

When one of the sisters had contracted cancer it had been a big news story. The media had followed her brave but ultimately unsuccessful battle against the disease. After her sister's death, however, the other sister had slowly faded from the headlines and returned to a less high profile life.

I am not particularly interested in attracting celebrity clients or rubbing shoulders with the rich and famous. I put as much care and effort into giving messages to the people sitting in the cheapest seats at the back of the theatre as I put into giving a message to the wealthy and powerful clients who come to see me privately. And there are plenty of them, I can tell you.

And so it was here. It didn't really matter to me that these sisters had once been household names or that I'd watched them on *Top of the Pops*.

I was simply glad that their sister act had been reformed, albeit all too briefly, and pleased to have given the one who remained in this life such a warm and loving message from the other side.

In doing that I was doing my job.

9

HOW THE SPIRITS CAN TRANSFORM YOU

'When you are born, you cry, and the world rejoices. When you die, you rejoice, and the world cries.' TIBETAN BUDDHIST SAYING

When we die, we are transformed: our spirits pass over to the other side. A new chapter begins in the story of our life.

Yet death can also transform the living.

It is one of the great ironies of death that while the personality of those who pass over doesn't change immediately, the personalities of those who are left behind can often alter quite dramatically. And sometimes, sadly, for the worse.

I have seen many cases where a widowed husband or wife has become unrecognisable from the person they were while their partner was alive. It is in many ways the greatest tragedy of death. And it is why none of us should let death be a disaster.

It is one of the most difficult lessons for us to understand, however. Fortunately, as I have learned over the years, the spirit world is close at hand to help us understand.

A Change Of Heart

'The greatest tragedy of life is not death, but what dies inside of us while we live.' NORMAN COUSINS

I have often tried to analyse why death affects us so much today. I think it's fair to say that we are more anxious about it now than people ever were in the past. It was very different in times gone by, partly I think because people had a better understanding of the fact that death is not the final act, that existence goes on beyond this earthly plane. People were also more comfortable with talking about the afterlife.

Today we live in a world where science is dominant. Too dominant, some would say. People want proof, tangible evidence of everything before they believe in it. Faith isn't enough any more for many people.

And yet I have noticed a curious thing about people who deny there is an afterlife, who say with scientific certainty: 'This is it, this is the only life we lead. After we die that's it, we're finished.' The strange thing is that they seem to experience more pain when they suffer a bereavement.

It's something I have seen consistently. Those who believe in the afterlife deal with loss much more easily than those who don't.

I had a friend, a lady I'll call Janet. Her husband David passed away at quite a young age in very sad circumstances. She was a very logical and scientific lady. She was absolutely adamant that there was no life after death.

I don't expect my friends to blindly believe in everything I do. I have many who are open-minded about my mediumship, and one or two who are out-and-out sceptics. It doesn't bother me. So as we spent time together during the weeks and months following her loss I didn't impose any of my views on her. I simply offered the hand of friendship and gave her the time and space she needed to grieve and move on.

In dealing with her grief, of course, she'd have her moments of anger and once or twice she hit out at me.

'David's dead, he's gone,' she'd say. 'And there's nothing anyone can do about it. Not even you, Colin.'

She'd always apologise afterwards.

What was frustrating for me as I looked on was the knowledge that this certainty she had wasn't actually helping her. In fact it was making life much more difficult for her. It was also transforming her personality.

In the weeks and months that followed her husband's passing I watched as she became a different person. She became quite bitter. She was adamant, for instance, that she wasn't going to remarry.

'I had my marriage—I don't want another partner; if I can't have the man that I wanted then I want nobody,' she would say.

Consequently she began to shut everybody out of her life and actually became quite a hard woman. She hadn't been like that before. When her husband had been alive she was a lively, effervescent, quite entertaining woman. She wouldn't have become my friend if she'd been the hard, acid-tongued person she'd now turned into.

Fortunately she was a very smart and instinctive person. And eventually she realised what was happening to her. Somehow she'd taken a good look at herself in the mirror and realised that she didn't like what she saw.

One day she asked me, very casually, about the

afterlife and what I thought happened after we pass over.

I was quite surprised but also pleased.

We soon found ourselves having a conversation in which I explained how I'd first come to believe in the spirit world and what evidence I'd been presented with to prove that there was an existence beyond this one. I talked about my grandfather and meeting Doris Stokes.

She was still sceptical, but at least she wasn't as dogmatic as she'd been before. After that she tentatively, almost reluctantly, started to look into it.

She started asking me questions whenever we met. She also went to see mediums. I had a very strong feeling that I shouldn't read for her, so I helped in recommending others that I felt would be right for her.

I spoke to her about the readings every now and again. She was positive without going overboard.

Slowly but surely she started to change. The old, effervescent personality began to re-emerge. And then one day I got a call from her. She was incredibly excited about the latest reading she'd had.

The medium had brought through her husband.

'At first I didn't believe her,' she told me. 'But then, Colin, she began coming up with all this detail.'

The medium told her how her husband was describing a tattoo he had done when he was a young man. 'David had it done when we were courting. We were only seventeen at the time,' Janet told me. 'We'd gone to Margate for the day and he'd had it done on the spur of the moment.

He'd had my name written on his upper arm. His parents went absolutely mad when they saw it.'

Until now she'd retained a little bit of scepticism about mediumship. A part of her hadn't quite made the leap of faith, she didn't believe in it one hundred per cent. The accuracy of this reading had changed all that.

'Even if she'd known he had a tattoo she couldn't have known the circumstances in which he got it,' she told me. 'The only people who knew about that were me and David. It must have been him there in the room. Colin, I never thought I'd experience anything like that in my life; it was absolutely unbelievable.'

The reading marked a turning point for her. Afterwards her transformation back into the warm-hearted, less cynical and generally happier person that she'd been before her husband's death continued.

After a couple of years she met another man, a really kind, intelligent guy with whom she got on very well. One day I got a phone call from her telling me that they were planning to get married.

'I know I said I'd never do it again, Colin, but that was then and this is now,' she said. 'Life has moved on.'

I felt strangely moved by the call. And I felt really proud of what she'd done in a very independent and clear-headed way. Afterwards she thanked me for the help I'd given her but that wasn't really necessary. I didn't really do anything. She'd simply remembered who she was. She then became the person her first husband had known and would have still wanted her to be. Once she'd achieved that her life had begun all over again.

Somewhere, I felt sure, David was proudly watching over her.

> 'If we were all created to be absolutely perfect in every single sense God would only have the need to have one woman and one man on the world at any given time. It's the fact that none of us is perfect that gives life such purpose.'
> MAGNUS, GUIDE TO COLIN FRY

I get bombarded by people via email and letters asking me to tell their loved ones that they miss them or that they are thinking of them. And my response is usually, 'Well, you can do that as well, you know.'

You can tell them that you miss them. You can also tell them that your life is moving on. And they will be pleased to hear it. What they won't be pleased to hear—or see—is that you have retreated into a shell.

Imagine a mother and daughter who are very close and the mother passes over. If that daughter becomes this person who is engrossed in misery, stops going out, grieves for her mother constantly and gets depressed, her mother is not going to be best pleased. If her mother was still on this side she would say get a grip of yourself. She'd say, 'This is not the person you are, I don't like seeing you like this, pull yourself together.'

Being a medium is a compassionate act; it's not a sympathetic act. In my opinion, one of the most misguided things we do is send cards 'in loving sympathy'. Sympathy disables, whereas compassion enables. Keep giving sympathy and it is like picking a scab: the wound never heals. As harsh as it might sound, if people look to me for sympathy they won't get it. Because as far as I'm concerned sympathy is no good to them whatsoever. But if they look to me for compassion then I have no problems with that.

SPIRIT SECRET

A question I'm often asked is, do our loved ones change when they pass over? Do they continue to grow in the spirit world? The answer is yes and no. We can hold whatever form we wish—young, old, or somewhere in between. In a physical sense the spirits are no longer shackled by their human forms so they do not grow in that way. But in a spiritual and emotional sense, then yes, as their existence continues so too does their evolution as spirits.

It doesn't happen immediately. We are on the other side for eternity so nothing has to happen quickly.

So to begin with our friends and loved ones who have passed over take all the old war wounds with them, all the strengths and flaws in their personality.

But change does happen over time.

The same, however, cannot always be said of those who are left behind. Often it is they who are most resistant to change.

Life always presents opportunities to turn a negative into a positive. And so it is with death.

People say all sorts of things in the heat of the emotional moments that follow someone's passing.

'I've got nothing left to live for.'

'My life will never be the same.'

'I don't know what to do now they've gone.'

These are all made as negative statements at the time. But in fact they can all be turned into a positive. And the key to that transition may lie in considering the person who has passed over.

So let's look at them one at a time.

'I've got nothing left to live for.' This is often said by a husband or wife when they lose their partner. My question to them is this: 'Are you saying that you did everything that you ever intended to do as a couple?' Did you make every trip, visit every country, see every West End show that you ever wanted to see? Of course you didn't. So why not turn a negative into a positive and do something that you didn't get round to with your partner?'

'My life will never be the same.' The short and simple answer to this is 'no, it won't'. How could it be? If you have lost the person to whom you were closest in the world, how can it be the same? It is by definition different. So why not celebrate that difference?

'I don't know what to do now they've gone.' Again the answer to this is simple. What would you have done if they hadn't gone? What would your life have entailed if you hadn't suffered your loss? Identify that and you've identified what to do next.

No matter how good a relationship might have been, whether it was between a mother and a child or a husband and a wife, or between friends, there are bound to have been things that were unfulfilled. A trip to a particular country or city that they never quite managed to organise? A visit to see someone perform whom they both loved? Whatever it might be, there is now a great opportunity. Not only does fulfilling your shared dream allow you to honour their memory and move your life on, it also brings you closer to the spirit of the person who has passed over.

I always admire people who can flip things around in this way. Rather than mourning the fact that they didn't do something with their partner, they go out and say, 'Right, I am going to do it now!'

Perhaps the most powerful reversal of this kind is parents who have lost a child. Their loss is of course huge and will never quite leave them. But I admire those who seize the opportunity to have another child, not as a replacement for the one they have lost but as a symbol of their ongoing love and to take the opportunity to parent another child.

Keeping It Real

Often, in order to have a meaningful relationship with the spirit world you have to accept some hard truths. And one of the hardest truths people have to face is the true nature of their relationship with those they have lost.

This is often a real barrier for people. I have come across countless people who, having lost a son or a daughter, a husband or a wife, a father or a mother, decide to completely reinvent that person when they pass over.

I remember a situation a few years back. I was in a conversation with someone who was talking about their husband. Now I knew her husband when he was alive and he was a vile man. He was a bully; I know he used to hit his wife during their marriage. But when he passed over she turned him into this idealised, perfect man. I would sit there shaking my head as she eulogised about what a wonderful, lovely man he had been, what a great father he had been. Yet in life none of this was true.

This is very common, unfortunately. Many people turn those who have passed over into saints when they are not. Equally a lot of people turn those they have lost into personalities that simply aren't recognisable as the person who lived and breathed on this earth.

Unless they realise what they are doing, these people have little chance of moving on with their lives.

'We are all damaged goods, but we don't have to be broken goods. Damaged goods keep functioning, broken goods don't.' MAGNUS, GUIDE TO COLIN FRY

Leading The Horse To Water

When they pass over to the other side, spirits go through a process where they evaluate who they are and what they have done in life. They face up to the reality of their earthly existence. They have to account for the way they have lived their life.

It's important that those who are left behind do the same thing. We must all face the truth. The spirit world understands this and does what it can to guide those who have been left behind along the right path. It doesn't always succeed, of course.

A few years ago I did a reading for a married pair. During the course of the reading it became clear that their son had experienced a traumatic passing. He had been murdered, stabbed on the way home from his local pub one night. The family had been terribly affected. It was now ten years since his death but it was obvious to me that the wounds had not fully healed.

His mother and father had come along to see me together, very much as a couple. I sensed early on that there was tension there, however. And immediately their son came through the cracks in their relationship began to appear.

When their son made himself known and began focusing his energy on his mother, the man made his displeasure clear. It was as if he was upset that he wasn't the first person with whom his son wanted to speak. At first he even denied it was his son.

As I began to deliver evidence, he kept shaking his head and muttering, 'That's not right, that's not right.'

Whenever he did so his wife would turn around and say, 'Yes it is, that's exactly right.'

At one point, for instance, I said to the mother that their son was quite involved with a local football team.

'He hated football,' his father said.

She snapped at this. 'He didn't like playing

football because you tried to force him to play it when he was a child, but he was on the entertainment committee at the club,' she said.

His father shook his head disapprovingly at this.

It then emerged that the son had been an entertainer of some kind and that his father had never approved of his choice of career.

The reading continued in this rather fractious, unhappy atmosphere for a few minutes more. The man continued to disagree with everything while at the same time his wife confirmed that it was correct.

By now, however, the father had become quite irritable and got up. 'I'd better leave, I'm obviously no good at this. I'm not being any help,' he said.

I felt the boy talking through me. He was angry. 'No, sit down Dad! That's always been your problem, you walked away from me all my life,' he said. The man looked shocked and, after a few moments, sat quietly and still.

The boy went on to explain that the reason his father didn't recognise these things that he was trying to communicate to his mother was that he had had no interest in him. He said his father had had no interest in his career during his life, no interest in him as a child. He only ever wanted him to be what he wanted him to be.

His mother confirmed it. 'You always wanted him to be something he wasn't. You were never there.'

Unfortunately, his father wasn't there much longer that day either. After a while he did what he had threatened to do by walking out and standing outside.

His wife was very apologetic about his

behaviour. 'He's never listened and he's not going to listen now,' she said.

I simply nodded. It was a reading that lived with me for a while afterwards because it illustrated something that I hadn't realised before.

The spirit of his son had made the effort to come through and speak to him. He had clearly evolved on the spirit side. He wanted to use his newfound wisdom to show his father the error of his ways. Yet his father had been unwilling—and perhaps unable—to listen to his son's message. He was probably never going to deal with the loss that he was obviously carrying with him ten years on.

It made me realise something: the spirit world is there to support and help us all. But it can only do so much. We have to do the rest. It reminded me of the old saying: you can lead a horse to water, but you cannot make it drink.

Megan's Law

When they suffer a distressing loss in life, people are left with a choice. They can continue to dwell on the awfulness of the tragedy. Or they can try to create something good out of that experience.

Time and again I have seen people turn the pain and negativity of their loss into a positive that has helped them not just get on with their lives but also honour the memory of the loved one they have lost.

One of the most common examples of this are parents who lose children and are then inspired to go on and work for charities dedicated to the causes of their child's death. This can range from charities dedicated to researching and finding a cure for diseases like cancer to campaigns raising awareness of social problems like knife crime. Not only is it admirable, I think it's also one of the best ways of dealing with the tragedy of loss.

I particulary remember the case of a lady in America, whose story I became fascinated by. Her name was Maureen Kanka and she lived in New Jersey.

Maureen suffered the worst thing that any parent can suffer when her seven-year-old daughter Megan was kidnapped, raped and murdered by a known sex offender named Jesse Timmendequas. He had been living in a house across the road from Maureen and her family, along with other convicted sex offenders. Yet Maureen had been completely unaware of the threat her neighbour represented.

The loss of her daughter was traumatic in the extreme. Maureen and her husband Richard were devastated. But in the dark days that followed, Maureen threw herself into a new cause.

Maureen and Richard started the Megan Nicole Kanka Foundation dedicated to changing the law so that 'every parent should have the right to know if a dangerous sexual predator moves into their neighbourhood'. The couple spent every waking hour promoting their cause. They circulated a petition which got more than 4,000 signatures.

Remarkably, within 89 days of Megan's death they had succeeded in persuading their home state of New Jersey to pass a law making it compulsory for communities to be notified of sex offenders who lived in their midst. The law was known as Megan's Law and became the model for similar laws across the United States.

I have encountered people like this elsewhere in the world—individuals who throw themselves into positive work rather than dwelling on the trauma of a loss. Closer to home, one of the most impressive of these people was a young man whose life had been turned upside down in really awful circumstances.

The teenage boy had still been at school when in a freak accident he had unintentionally stabbed and killed one of his best friends. The courts had shown little sympathy for his plea of manslaughter. He had been given a heavy jail sentence.

His time in jail had been awful for him. He suffered terrible, terrible guilt. I was contacted by a member of his family who was desperate to help ease his pain.

I did a reading during which the boy he had stabbed came through. His message was one of reconciliation and forgiveness. He told his friend to get on with his life. I have mentioned this boy's story before. But I mention it again because what he did after eventually leaving prison is very relevant here.

The lad managed to put his past behind him and make a new life for himself. And he did so by turning the negativity of his previous life into something positive for the future. He is now very active in educating children in why you shouldn't carry knives. It is an example of how you can turn a negative into a positive. And once again, the spirit world had played its part in making it happen.

10.

HOW THE SPIRITS CAN BEFRIEND YOU

'Sit down before fact like a little child, be prepared to give up every preconceived notion, follow humbly to wherever and to whatever abysses nature leads, or you shall learn nothing.' THOMAS HUXLEY

The spirit world is close by at all times. And yet some people are unable—or unwilling—to acknowledge its presence. I am frequently asked by sceptics for some kind of proof that the afterlife exists. Some are desperate for evidence.

I remember one very highly qualified academic saying to me: 'Look, I've read every single book there is to read on this subject and yet I've not had a single experience that persuades me that there is something beyond this life.'

I had to break the bad news to him. I had to tell him that he hadn't found anything because all he'd done was sit down and read books.

Evidence doesn't come to you, you have to go out and look for it. You have to sit in halls watching demonstrations, join circles and have private readings. Some are going to be exceptional, some are going to be downright awful. But little bits of information will trickle out about how people's consciousness has survived this thing called physical death. And when you add them all up over the years, those little bits of evidence build up into a fuller picture.

Of course, it isn't always such a long-drawn-out process. The spirit world is often very eager to prove its existence. And it can do so in dramatic fashion, as I have discovered many times during the course of my thirty-plus years as a medium.

Maggie and Julia

Part of my mission in life is to spread the message about the afterlife to as large an audience as possible. The great beauty of performing in large auditoria in front of hundreds, sometimes thousands, of people is that it provides me with an ideal opportunity to spread that message. Some people need more convincing of the presence of an afterlife than others. For these people, simple faith isn't enough. They need hard, incontrovertible evidence. I don't have any problem with that at all. I welcome people who are sceptical just as long as they have an open mind.

Often there are a fair few sceptics or doubters scattered around these audiences and I take it as a matter of extreme pride that I have spoken to many who have left my shows having been persuaded to think again.

One case that always sticks in my memory happened at a performance in the Midlands. I remember it because the sceptic was a member of my production team rather than the audience.

It was a few hours before an evening performance and, along with the crew who put together my shows, I was doing the routine sound and lighting check that I perform before all my demonstrations.

There were a lot of microphones on around the

auditorium. My tour manager overheard a girl and another member of the crew talking about me and what I did in a really derogatory manner. He went over to them and said, 'We're really not interested in your opinion of Colin. You're paid to do a job and I suggest you get on with it.' It was very embarrassing, in particular for the girl who'd been making the remarks. She looked absolutely mortified to have been discovered like this. She couldn't stop apologising and her face was as red as a beetroot.

I thought nothing more about it until the show that night. Early on during the demonstration I got a message from a woman called Julia who was looking for her former partner—another woman. 'She's trying to connect to another lady who had a very close bond with her,' I said.

Perhaps unsurprisingly, a few people shifted uncomfortably around in their chairs. It didn't seem like anyone in the audience was prepared to identify themselves as gay—despite the fact that the man on the stage did so many years ago. I wasn't prepared to let this connection go simply to spare someone's blushes, however.

As I tried to locate the person Julia was trying to connect to in the auditorium I kept finding myself being directed towards the back of the theatre where the sound and lighting crew were at work. 'I'm trying to connect to a lady called Maggie. Is there anyone who understands that?' I asked.

Again there was a long, deathly silence. But then I saw a hand slowly rising. To my amazement, it was that of the girl my manager had torn a strip off earlier in the day.

'I'm seeing that she is not a relation but a close

friend of yours,' I said.

'Yes, that's right, we were partners,' she said, speaking rather nervously into the microphone.

I sensed the relief in Julia's energy but I also sensed pain. 'She's also showing me a car, a small car and an accident,' I said.

'I understand what you mean,' Maggie said.

'I can see an articulated lorry, being driven by a foreign driver. He is tired and confused and sways over to the wrong side of the road. Before he can do anything he has driven head on into the car.'

'Yes, she died in an accident,' the girl said, close to tears. 'She was driving her Mini and she was hit, head on, by an articulated lorry.'

'She is now showing me that you weren't happy with the inquest into her death,' I said. 'You thought it was a whitewash.'

'No, I wasn't,' the girl confirmed. She said she'd wanted the driver of the lorry to be punished more severely.

I could see the anger she still felt about this but Julia had a message for her.

'She says you must get over it,' I told her. 'She says you must drop this thing you have about getting this man punished for what happened.'

By now Maggie was in tears and shaking. 'Yes, I will,' she said quietly.

At the end of the show Maggie came up to see me. I could see from the look on her face that she was embarrassed, this time for another reason.

'I am so sorry, Colin,' she said. 'I always thought what you did was a load of nonsense really. But you told me things that you couldn't possibly have known. There were details that only Julia and I knew.'

Her ex-partner was trying to get her to move on in her life.

Two Birds With One Stone

One night, a few years ago, I was doing a demonstration at a theatre in the North Wales seaside town of Rhyl. Towards the end of the evening I felt myself in the presence of a young woman. I sensed immediately that she had a very particular message she wanted to pass on. She was also directing me very specifically towards a certain part of the theatre.

'I need to come up to you, my love—I have your daughter with me and she is showing me that her name is Sandra. She is showing me that she spoke to you specifically on three occasions today,' I said.

'At 10.25 am, 2.10 pm and 4.05 pm.'

The lady I was speaking to didn't say anything.

'My love, I understand that you did this because you wanted to see if she could respond to you. And you've written these times on a piece of paper that you have in your handbag,' I said.

She looked shocked at this.

'And you have something else in the bag—your daughter's toy which you were holding in your hand at the times you wrote down.'

At this she leant down and reached for her handbag. She then produced a little teddy bear from inside.

'This was Sandra's favourite toy,' she said, her voice quivering.

She then produced a little, scrunched-up piece of paper.

'Could you open it up and show it to the

audience, my love?' I asked.

When she did so the audience let out a gasp of amaze ment. On it were scrawled three times: 10.25 am, 2.10 pm and 4.05 pm. The audience burst into a massive round of applause. They were delighted, as indeed I was, but for more reasons than one.

The funny thing about that particular reading was that it killed two birds with one stone, so to speak. The person who had handed her the microphone that evening was my new manager, Eden. We had been friends for six months before we began working together, but he had always been sceptical about what I did. 'I don't actually believe in what you do but I'm prepared to keep an open mind,' he'd said to me.

This was the first night that he'd been on tour with me and he had said he wanted to get a feel for what I was doing that night, so he'd been helping out by passing the microphones around the auditorium.

When this message had come through for the lady sitting near him, Eden said that all the hairs on the back of his neck stood up.

'That was the point when you convinced me,' he said afterwards. 'I'd been with you all day. We'd been shopping together. I know there is no conceivable way that you could have got that information.'

It's giving evidence that they are aware of us and that their living consciousness has carried on. That's what people are looking for when they come for a communication. They want to know that people have carried on, that they still exist and are still sentient beings.

SPIRIT SECRET

My spirit guide Magnus has a favourite saying—'A wise man once said, "I think therefore I am," but it can be reversed. I am, so I had better think.'

It says in the Bible that God created man in his own image. There are few in the world today who would believe that they look like God and in that they are right. But there is truth in the Scriptures. God created us by thought and we were created to think. Therefore God does exist in all of us.

I Told You So

Another question I get asked quite often is this; what happens to those who don't believe in the afterlife? Do they pass over to the same spirit dimension? And, assuming they do inhabit the spirit realm, do sceptics ever come through with messages?

Many people are surprised to hear this, but the answer to both questions is a definite yes.

I had witnessed examples of this in demonstrations I'd watched as a younger man. But the first time it happened to me was at a reading I did back in the 1990s.

The reading was with a middle-aged lady. She was clearly an intelligent woman, quite well educated. She wasn't exactly aloof, but she wasn't very warm either. To be honest, at first I thought her slightly cold attitude might deter any spirits from coming through. No sooner had I begun the reading, however, than I felt myself in the presence of a man. He too was clearly an intelligent person.

183

He didn't mince his words either.

'I wouldn't have liked you much when I was alive,' he said to me. 'I didn't believe in what you do. To be honest, I thought it was a load of old nonsense.'

I didn't argue with him. I didn't need to. I think I'd proven my point.

As the connection settled down it became clear to me that he'd been this lady's partner in life. 'I need to communicate with her,' he kept saying to me. 'She believed really strongly that there was something on the other side. And I promised to tell her if there really was.'

It took me some time to persuade her that it was really him. But I eventually produced all the evidence she needed to be convinced.

'See—I was right,' she said, quite emotional by now.

She left the reading transformed, hugging me as she said goodbye and chattering away happily about how pleased she was to discover her husband's spirit was living on.

In some ways, such readings are more satisfying than those for 'believers'.

Bullseye

I had a similar experience when I did a reading for the television presenter Dr David Bull. He was a sceptic who because of his scientific background simply couldn't accept what I did unless there was evidence to prove it. To his credit, however, he was willing to have a reading.

He was, like so many others who come to me with a doubting mind, very careful not to give anything away. He didn't respond to my words and tried his best to keep facial movements to a minimum. He was convinced that otherwise his body language would give something away.

He was, of course, missing the point. Quite quickly I felt myself in the presence of a very strong character, a youngish man who had passed over not very long before. I felt that he had suffered with a pain around his neck and throat area towards the end.

'He went through his final days in denial,' I said. 'Even though he knew there was something very wrong with him.'

David smiled occasionally as I continued communicating with this man.

'This was a man who people either loved or loathed,' I went on. 'On the one hand he is quite a loud person. But he is also someone who didn't like being seen in the limelight in some ways. He did a lot of work for charity but he didn't like people making a fuss of it.'

David clearly knew who was communicating with him but continued to say nothing.

As he faded, the man said something rather profound. 'He is telling me that some friendships are meant for ever,' I said.

Afterwards David admitted on camera that he knew who I was talking about. One of his friends, called Mark, had died of cystic fibrosis. It was clear that they had been incredibly close.

David admitted that he himself had sensed that Mark was going to die. He told how, while driving up the motorway to film a television programme one evening, he was struck by an overwhelming feeling that he would never see his friend Mark again.

He said that he pulled into a service station and wrote a letter which he then faxed through to Mark. It was probably one of the last things Mark read because he died very soon afterwards.

David said that I'd been 'right on the spot' in many of my observations about Mark. He said that Mark was someone who polarised people enormously. If he thought someone was talking rubbish he would tell them so.

It was the final thought that really hit him, however. He admitted that he found the idea of their friendship being one that would last for ever 'beautiful'. He conceded that he talked more about Mark than he did about friends who were still alive. So Mark's final comment had been 'rather beautiful'.

The reading wasn't enough to completely change David's mind. But it was enough for him to admit afterwards that some of the things I said were 'too close'. 'Maybe . . .' he said.

And that was more than enough for me.

11.

HOW THE SPIRITS CAN REWARD YOU

'Sometimes the worst answer to your prayer would be to give you that for which you asked.' SILVER BIRCH THROUGH THE MEDIUMSHIP OF MAURICE BARBANELL

Give And You Shall Receive

The spirit world has taught me a great deal. Some of the lessons I have learned have been simple, others much more profound.

The most important lesson, of course, has been that there is more to life than this earthly existence, that death is not the end. But the other really important thing my mediumship has shown me is that we can all achieve the things we want on this earthly plane. Provided, that is, that we live our lives according to the quite simple and straightforward principles by which the universe works.

If anybody ever says to me, 'What is the big secret of life?' I always answer the same way. It's this: that God, the Supreme Being, the Creator, or whatever you want to call the force that oversees the universe, will give you whatever you want, as long as you know why you want it, what you are going to do with it and what you are going to put back afterwards.

It's not a new idea. Far from it. It pre-dates Christianity and other religions. It's actually the idea behind some of the supposedly new philosophies that are summed up in books like *The Secret* and ideas like the Cosmic Ordering Service.

I don't give it a fancy name. I just call it the law of acquisition. And it applies as much to the way that you draw on the spirit world for help as it applies to any other aspect of life. I know this is true because I have experienced it many times myself.

SPIRIT SECRET
When it comes to looking for spirit guidance in life you can put out the plea to the spirit world, 'Help me,' but the response is always going to be: 'What do you want us to help you with?' Be specific.

The Law Of Acquisition

The first time I understood this was when I was in my early twenties. I'd been living with my parents but wanted my own space, my own home. So I put my name down on the local council housing list.

After a while I was impatient because I hadn't been offered a flat. I went down to the housing office and complained. The poor chap that I harangued looked at me as if I was mad. 'You're a single man. Do you have any idea how long the waiting list is for a council house? There are so many people ahead of you in the queue, you could still be waiting for a house in six years' time,' he said, shaking his head almost pityingly.

My usual attitude at that age was to refuse to take no for an answer. So I refused to leave until he came up with an idea.

'Well, there is something we might be able to offer you,' he eventually said.

'Oh yes,' I said. 'What's that?'

'Well there's a thing called the shared ownership scheme where you buy the house in partnership with the council,' he said. My eyes lit up. At that point I'd never thought of owning my own property. I had nothing put by for a deposit so I set myself a year to save the money I needed to get this house.

I got myself a second part-time job as a cleaner. For a while I was getting up at the crack of dawn and cleaning offices from 5 am to 8 am; going home, getting showered and going to my day job as a floor manager in a department store; and then working three nights a week at a pub. I saved and I saved and I saved because I had a very specific goal. Unfortunately, that's all I had—a goal. I hadn't thought through why I wanted to reach that goal. I didn't understand the law of acquisition.

Soon I had enough for a deposit and I found this little house. I was in such a hurry to get a house—any house—that I charged at the situation like a bull at a gate. And so it was that I moved into a little two-bedroom 1970s starter home.

I moved in with very little. Apart from a fridge that a relative had given me, all I had was a beanbag, a sleeping bag and a new pussycat. And once I'd finished decorating it I realised I was living in a glorified rabbit hutch. All I could think was how much I hated it. I didn't want to be there. Because it was a little terraced house you could hear everything from the flushing of the neighbours' loo to their Saturday-night lovemaking!

Things went from bad to worse. Soon after moving in I was made redundant. I rushed into getting another job, but again didn't think about it. That was the theme of my life at the time. I was rushing into things that I later regretted. I wasn't thinking things through.

Fortunately, however, I had the spirits guiding me. And they began to show me the light.

At the time I was very much into reading about positive thinking. One day I decided to completely change the way I was thinking. I was doing well as a medium during my spare time and could see that if I had the right set-up I could even think about doing it professionally. I also knew that having a home in which I was happy and contented would help me achieve that goal. Living in my rabbit hutch wasn't going to help me.

So I gave myself this pep talk. For months I had listened to myself making all these excuses: 'I can't move because I'm not earning enough money, I can't afford a bigger mortgage.' I told myself that this was going to stop right now and that I was going to motivate myself by thinking positively rather than negatively.

I started by telling myself that I'd been here before. When I'd wanted my first home I'd worked myself to a standstill and got the money I needed. I could do it again.

The difference was that this time I knew why I wanted it and I knew what I was going to give back when I got it. I wanted it so that I could be happy and motivated. And I was going to give something very valuable back through my mediumship.

It altered things almost immediately.

A couple of days after I'd given myself my pep

talk I was driving up the road and saw a 'For Sale' board. I looked at the lovely semi-detached house and saw that it was precisely the kind of house that, in my mind's eye, I had imagined myself living in. Immediately I thought: 'That's my house, that's the house I want.'

I slammed on the brakes and pulled the car over. I then rang the estate agent on the number on the board.

'How much is this house on the market for?' I asked.

They gave me the price and I took a sharp intake of breath.

'OK,' I said.

'When would you like to view it?' the estate agent asked.

'Now,' I said.

After I had seen it I went back home. I put an offer in there and then.

I had a partner at the time who I was living with. When I told him about the house he asked to see it too. Afterwards, he agreed it was perfect. 'The only thing is, Colin, where are you going to get the money to pay for it?' he said.

He was right in one sense. The money I was going to get for selling my share in the rabbit hutch wasn't going to be enough to cover the deposit that I needed to get the mortgage I wanted.

I decided to ask the spirit world for help. I put it out to the spirit world that I wanted this to happen. The law of acquisition was soon working on my behalf.

The next day, completely out of the blue, I got a phone call from someone I knew within the spiritualist movement.

'Colin, I've just had a very unexpected phone call,' he said. 'How would you like to go out to Finland to do some demonstrations? They want to pay you for it.'

'Really,' I said. 'How much?'

The amount of money they were offering was almost exactly the shortfall I needed to buy the new house.

I couldn't quite believe it. It had worked.

I was due two weeks' holiday from work so I headed off to Finland a few days later. In the meantime the housing association sold the old house, the purchase of the new house went through and I got exactly what I wanted.

It was proof of the law of acquisition. Wanting wasn't enough. Moaning about it wasn't enough. I had to change my approach. I had stopped moaning and complaining about the situation I was in and I had decided to do something about it. As soon as I did that, the impossibilities of the situation melted away.

It was when I got to Finland that the reality of what had happened really hit home. I had been asked to go over to give a series of private sittings, séances and trance demonstrations. The trip was being organised by the Finnish Spiritualist Society and was being hosted by families, which was very nice. My friend Patricia came with me and we stayed with two very lovely families out there.

For the last part of the tour we stayed with a lady in Helsinki. She was going to stay with her sister and she was letting us have her flat while she was away. However, she was still there when Patricia and I arrived.

When I met the lady I could sense immediately

that she was someone who had been through a difficult period in her life. I sensed that she might be the reason I'd been invited out to Finland. I also sensed that this might be one of the things I was going to be asked to do in return for being given what I wanted.

I put it out to the spirit world and they responded immediately. As the lady was getting ready to leave I told her that I'd received a message. We sat down and I did a reading for her.

I had got a strong sense that her mother was with me. 'She is telling me that she has a message for you and your sister,' I said.

The lady was very pleased by this.

I sensed that her mother hadn't passed over long ago. I think she'd been gone something like two years.

As the sitting continued I got the strong feeling that this lady had been leaving her flat, the way she was today, a lot during the final years of her mother's life. She confirmed that her mother had been in and out of hospital those last years. She and her sister had taken it turns to go and spend time with her.

They were both retired ladies so their mother must have been quite elderly. But they'd been determined that she wouldn't go into a nursing home.

It turned out that the lady had been trying to make a connection with her mother for more than two years. She'd been to all sorts of gatherings in Helsinki and further afield in Finland. She'd sat in circles and had private one-on-one sittings with leading mediums there, but to no avail. She'd not been able to make contact. She had become a little disillusioned and rather sad about it.

'You don't know how happy you've made me,' she said after the sitting. 'I didn't know whether to ask you for a sitting as I didn't think it was quite the right thing to do.'

When she'd left and I was alone in her flat with Pat, I sat down and thought about it. This hadn't happened by chance. There was nothing random about the communication I'd passed on.

Even though I'd passed on several important and powerful messages while I was in Finland, it felt to me that this was the one that I had come here specifically to deliver. This was the price I had to pay for having got what I wanted back in England. It was the first time that I had seen the power of the law of acquisition. Since then I have followed it diligently.

I absolutely believe that everything in life is about deciding what you want, knowing why you want it, knowing what you are going to do with it and what you are going to put back. It's to me the secret of a successful and positive life.

The powers-that-be—whether they be guides, angels, God or whatever it is you believe in— cannot respond until you've made that decision. Then they will make things happen for you. But it has to be by your will and through your decision.

In this particular case I had visualised the house that I wanted to live in. I had made affirmations in my mind of what the perfect house was. I wanted a three-bedroom, semi-detached house and I wanted it to be a Victorian house because I was fed up with living in a new property. I wanted it to have a basement and a big kitchen and an open fireplace. I had visualised it entirely.

194

That offer to go out to work in Finland had probably always been waiting there for me. But I had to start the process off that led me there.

It's a lesson we can all learn from.

The only answer I can give to someone who says 'nothing good happens in my life' is 'yes, you are absolutely right, because that's what you've decided'.

Gods, angels, whatever. None of these things can help you until you use the one thing we've all been given and that is free will. You have to do it yourself. You have to apply the law of acquisition.

Finding The Right Help

Finding my perfect home was far from the last time the law of acquisition worked for me. A couple of years after I moved house, I needed to fix something else in my life.

By this time I was becoming a very well known medium in the spiritualist community. I was working full-time. I still had my part-time job working as a barman three nights a week in a pub. At the same time I was trying to fit in the ever-increasing demand for me to do demonstrations.

One of the gifts I have never developed is omnipresence: I can't be in two places at the same time!

One night I inadvertently double-booked. I was incredibly embarrassed by this. I sat down and said, 'I'm going to need some help with this, I can't do this on my own. I need someone to manage me.' So once again I put it out to the spirit world. I knew what I wanted and why I wanted it. I also knew exactly what I was going to give back in return.

195

Within a very short space of time I cultivated a friendship with a guy called Vince, who helped me voluntarily for a while but eventually became my manager, travelling around the country with me.

He helped me with my bookings and travelling arrangements. He made sure that I didn't double-book myself again. He has remained a great friend.

Something similar happened years later when I needed another kind of influence to guide me in my career. I was in my late twenties and my work as a medium was really taking off in a big way. At the time I was a member of a Spiritualist Society called the Noah's Ark Society. I really wanted the company of an elder statesman in the community. I had this feeling that because so many of my older friends had passed over I was lacking that kind of influence in my life. And I wasn't yet old enough to be that kind of figure to someone else. I just knew I could really do with an older friend.

I did my first demo at the Noah's Ark Society and there was a gent there called George Cranley. He came over and introduced himself.

'I have heard quite a bit about you, young man,' he said. 'Most of it quite good.' He looked over his glasses and added, 'But if I don't think you are very good I shall have no hesitation in telling you.'

I just thought he was the most rude and arrogant old curmudgeon. But over quite a short period of time he became one of my closest friends and he also became a mentor.

He has been a great supporter of my work. He's toured with me on lecture tours. He did two Australian tours and he also came with me on that trip to Japan in 1999 at the invitation of the Japanese Spiritualist Society. When I first acquired a college in Sweden he helped me co-ordinate it and helped me tutor out there.

I hope I can pick up the phone to him at any time.

He's not universally popular and over the years a number of people have tried to break our friendship. But I choose my friends—I don't have them chosen for me—and George and his wife both remain amongst my dearest friends.

Again he came into my life at a time I was thinking that I really could do with a mentor—someone that I could learn from.

Once again I had put it out there to the universe and I had been rewarded with what I needed and wanted.

A Spiritual Argos Catalogue

A lot has been written by other people about the law of acquisition in recent years. It's the principle behind ideas like the Cosmic Ordering Service, which has been very much in vogue for a few years now. It's also the 'secret' contained in the bestselling book *The Secret*. I am not a huge fan of most of these approaches. I think they cheapen the spirituality of the idea. They also encourage people to use the law in an irresponsible way, failing to emphasise the payback aspect enough.

The important thing to remember is that it's not a spiritual Argos catalogue. Every single thing that you seek and ask for in life has a payback price. And that payback price has to be something you are prepared to do and are also willing to do. You have to be sure that you understand what is being asked of you before you apply this.

Let me give you a good example. Years ago I had a colleague, a female medium, with whom I was acquainted. As a medium she was absolutely brilliant. She had a wonderful ability to understand and interpret the spirit world. But she was a curious contradiction in many ways.

You have to be quite strong psychologically to do this job, but she wasn't. I have long thought that there are some people who have the gift yet should perhaps leave it alone. She was one of them.

Her emotional life had become quite complicated. She had originally been married to the great love of her life but he had died, leaving her to bring up her children alone. Not long afterwards her daughter had a child at a very young age so she was effectively left to bring up her granddaughter as well.

In the wake of her husband's passing she'd had a string of disastrous relationships. She kept asking the universe to provide her with someone to love but she had only succeeded in attracting a succession of totally unsuitable men.

She reached a particularly low ebb at one point and went to see another medium. What happened next is another warning about taking predictive messages as absolute truth. She was told that a man was going to come from foreign shores and his initials would be BK.

Within a short period of time she'd met a man called Bernard Kendricks. They had a whirlwind romance and got married within weeks of meeting each other. What is it they say?—marry in haste, repent at leisure? Well, these two were totally unsuitable for each other.

She realised this very shortly into the marriage.

She tried very hard to love him but she didn't get back what she wanted from their relationship. Again, it was an example of being very specific about what you ask for in life. She'd got what she'd asked for—someone to love—but not someone to love her back.

Her unhappiness at this was compounded when, a few months after being married, she attended a seminar at a college of further education near her home. The course was a real tonic for her, in particular because of the mix of like-minded people there.

Among those she befriended was a very smart and warm guy named Brian Kim. It was only on the final day of the seminar that she actually got to know his name. The moment she discovered it she realised her mistake: she had married the wrong BK.

The good news for her was that she was able to correct the mistake. Her friendship with Brian turned out to be the real thing and her marriage to Bernard was dissolved by mutual consent before they had even celebrated their first wedding anniversary.

Her experience underlines an important truth about the law of acquisition, however. The universe will give you what you want but you have to think it through properly. It means being clear about what you want and being clear about making the commitment—even if you don't know at the time what it is you're supposed to put back.

The Tale Of The Stonecutter

One of the most apposite and beautiful stories I have

read in recent years was told by the writer Benjamin Hoff in his bestselling book *The Tao of Pooh*.

Hoff tells the tale of a humble stonecutter who was dissatisfied with his status in life. One day, the stonecutter walked by the house of a wealthy merchant and saw it filled with beautiful things and important visitors. He felt envious of the merchant and his power and wished he could be like him.

To his amazement, his wish came true and he was instantly transformed into the merchant, surrounded by fine things and people. He was also envied and detested in equal measure.

It wasn't long, however, before he was dissatisfied. One day he saw a high-ranking official passing by his house in a sedan chair that was being carried by servants. Everyone was bowing to the official.

'I wish I was as powerful as that, I wish I could be that official,' he thought to himself.

Before he knew it, he had become the official and was being carried around in the sedan chair with people bowing and scraping in his presence. He was feared and hated.

Suddenly, however, he felt very hot. The sun was blazing in the sky and as he looked up to it he was struck by how unaffected it was by his presence.

He wished that he could be the sun.

Once more he was transformed—this time into the sun—and began shining down on everyone below. For a while he shone down fiercely, scorching the fields and being cursed by the farmers. But then a giant dark cloud appeared, blocking the earth's view of him. His light could no longer shine down.

'How powerful that cloud is,' he thought, and he

wished to be like it.

Immediately he was transformed into the cloud and he burst into a fierce rainstorm that flooded the fields and villages, much to the anger of the people below.

Soon, however, he found his power was being removed as the wind pushed him away.

'How I wish I was as powerful as the wind,' he thought. Soon he had been transformed yet again and was blowing tiles of the roofs of houses and uprooting trees, to the horror of the people.

But then he came into contact with a huge, towering stone. No matter how hard he tried to blow, he could not move it.

What a powerful force that stone is, he thought to himself. I wish I could be like that stone.

Once again he was transformed and for a while he thought himself more powerful than anything else on earth. But then he felt the force of a hammer driving a chisel into the stone and he found himself being changed.

'What force could be more powerful than me, than stone?' he asked himself.

He looked down from on high, and far below him on the ground he saw the figure of a humble stonecutter.

12.

HOW THE SPIRITS CAN FREE YOU

'Man was born to be free, to dwell in liberty.
He was not born to be a slave, bound and
fettered. His life should be full of richness, the
richness of mind and body and spirit. All
knowledge should be open to him, all truth,
all wisdom, all inspiration. He should dwell in
the splendour of the spirit with none of the
cramping, irksome, vexatious restrictions
imposed upon him by those who would deny
his heritage and thwart his destiny.' SILVER
BIRCH

I've got quite strong views on how and when and if
mediums should get involved in investigating crimes.
I've been involved in about fifty cases over the years.
It's never something that I willingly get involved in.
I have never, ever rung up the police and said I had
some information for them.

I've always taken the position that I am in the
public domain and if they want to approach me
and ask for my help then they can do so. But I
reserve the right to decline to help. There have
been situations where I've said the people
concerned were better off leaving it to the police to
conduct their investigations. The situations I'm
most happy to get involved in are those where the
families ask for help.

It is here that I am fulfilling my role as a
medium by helping to free both the victims and

their families from the anger and sense of injustice they so often feel at their loss. Doing so can also help right the wrongs that have caused their pain.

A Walk In The Forest

It all began in the 1980s when I did a reading for the wife of a senior police officer. It was a perfectly normal sitting and quite a successful one. She was very pleased with it, or so I thought.

When, a few days later, I got a phone call from her husband I was at first slightly alarmed. He introduced himself as a senior Chief Inspector at one of the main constabularies in the south of England. He sounded like he was calling on official business.

A hundred thoughts rushed through my head. Why was he calling me? Had my reading with his wife not gone as well as I'd imagined? Had I taxed the car?!

He soon put my mind at rest. 'Look,' he said. 'My wife speaks very highly of you and I have read about you in the press. I don't know if this is something that you would be prepared to become involved in, but there's something that we'd like you to have a look at.'

I was intrigued so I simply said yes.

'This is all strictly off the record, of course, but we've got a very peculiar murder that's just taken place. The crime scene is still open and I could arrange for you to be taken there. Would you be interested in coming and having a look for us?'

I felt slightly torn. On the one hand I was reluctant to step into the world of professional criminal investigation. I knew there were one or two mediums who worked in this area but I'd heard mixed reports about how they were treated by some detectives. The Chief Inspector sounded very respectful of what I did, but would all his junior officers feel the same way? Did I want to get into that? But on the other hand I couldn't help but be intrigued. I also felt confident that the spirit world would help me.

So, after a moment or two of hesitation, I made a decision. 'OK. I can't promise I'll give you anything useful but I'm happy to try to help,' I said.

'Thank you, Mr Fry. I'll get someone to give you a call to arrange for you to get to the crime scene tonight,' he said.

Later that evening I drove over to an area of forest about half an hour from my home. The scene of the crime was still cordoned off with police tape and I was told to head towards the floodlights that were illuminating an area inside the woods.

A rather surly-looking PC had been assigned to accompany me. I could tell he didn't think much of having to 'babysit' a psychic medium and he wasted no time in confirming it. As he was walking me down through this wood, the constable basically started taking the mickey out of me.

I just turned to him and smiled. 'When you get home tonight you're going to have a hell of a mess to clear up,' I said.

He looked shocked. 'What do you mean by that?'

'Well, when you had that row with your wife this morning before you left for work and you threw your breakfast across the kitchen, your wife left it there. And if you want to know where your wife and your two children are, they're at her mother's house. And you'll be damned lucky if they ever come back.'

He went very quiet. 'OK, you've proved your point,' he said.

'Remember, I didn't ask to come here, I was invited.'

He didn't say another word as we made our way down to the crime scene.

I had been given more of a briefing on the crime by the officer who had called me to arrange the visit to the forest. A male body had been found in the woods. The hands, feet and head had been taken off. All they had was a torso with nothing identifiable on it. The body itself had now been taken away but it was still a pretty grisly scene with splashes of blood dotted around the woodland.

Working psychically I began to concentrate on the evidence that was around me. After a while I began to pick up on a series of images that someone—I didn't know who—was showing me.

I told the officers at the scene that I could see a house on the High Street of a local village. It was either 33 or 37. What I did know was that the house was vacant.

'Whatever this is all about, there is a clue at the bottom of the well in the back garden of this house,' I said.

By now it was approaching four or five in the morning. I had been there all night with them. This was a serious investigation, however, so there was no time to think about sleep. We jumped straight in a squad car and headed to the village I'd seen in my mind.

As I'd predicted, when we got to the street we

discovered that both number 33 and 37 were vacant. I sensed immediately that it was number 37 that we should be concentrating on. We gained entry to the house, then made our way into the garden.

At first the police could find no evidence of a well. They were about to give up when I spotted a statue in the corner of the garden.

'There's a well under there,' I said.

When they moved the statue and dragged off the large paving slab that had been lying underneath, a hole revealed itself. Sure enough it was a well.

And when they shone their torchlights down there they found a load of videotapes floating in the water.

'Whatever they are, it plays a huge part in explaining why this guy was murdered,' I said.

I also came up with two names for them.

I remained in contact with the team investigating the murder for a while afterwards. 'It's highly likely that you're right,' they told me.

It transpired that when they examined the videos they contained child pornography. They were working on the theory that the crime was connected to two guys who were involved in the Russian Mafia. They had been tailing the pair for some time but every time they got close to them they moved on. They would leave the country and become untraceable.

Their hunch was that this guy had been a runner for them, distributing this extreme pornography. He had been fiddling them financially and had been pocketing some of the money that belonged to them.

To punish him and to send a message out to anyone else that worked with them, they had killed the guy. The difficulty for the police was that his body was completely unidentifiable. There were no dental records, no fingerprints, nothing to go on.

I remained on good terms with the officers on the case, although at one point there was a misunderstanding that almost got me arrested. Two of the police officers couldn't understand how I could possibly have known so much based on what I'd seen. 'We might need to question you more about this,' they said to me at the station one day.

Fortunately the Chief Inspector had been nearby. 'Don't be so bloody stupid, that's what I brought him in for, this is what he does,' he told them.

At the time they couldn't prove anything I was saying. But I learned quite recently that the body has been exhumed. I have also been told that some of the things they couldn't understand when I raised them years ago now begin to make a bit more sense. With the benefit of DNA evidence, the mystery of the torso in the forest might finally be solved.

One of the things I was told at the very outset of the investigation was that the police would deny my involvement if they were ever asked about it. I remember a detective taking me to one side.

'We will not be able to publicly acknowledge that you have been working with us. And I need to explain to you why,' he said. 'First of all, we have to find the physical evidence to corroborate whatever you say. If we are ever asked about any work that you did for us we will have to say that it came to nothing. We have to say that,' he said.

'Secondly, if you are working on a case where the murderer is still at large, if you are spouting your mouth off about what you're picking up on and presenting it publicly, you are potentially setting yourself up as a target for that murderer to silence you.'

It's a position that causes me no problems at all. There are some mediums who write books and put the work they've done with the police in the public domain. I suspect that they may sometimes just be doing it for their own glory and I think they are potentially damaging police investigations. I wouldn't dream of doing that. What's important is catching the perpetrator—not making sure that you get the publicity that lets everyone know you were involved.

Since then I have developed quite strong views on how, when and if mediums should get involved in investigating crimes.

Bodies Of Evidence

To do some parts of my job you've got to be pretty steely and determined. As a medium it's important when you start getting involved in things like this that you realise there is going to be subtle intimidation at times. You will be told not to pursue certain avenues.

But the spirits are always close by. The truth will always come out through them—even if it doesn't then make it into the wider world.

Filming the television series *Psychic Private Eyes* was a demanding and testing time for me for all sorts of reasons. The cases we were presented with were difficult and sometimes harrowing. But there was also a real sense that we were interfering in areas that the authorities would rather we didn't.

The main reason I agreed to do the series was that the friends or families of murder victims had asked me to become involved. Once I knew that I had their approval I also knew that the spirits of those who had passed over would make sure that we weren't deflected from our goals. And I was proven right.

Two cases stand out. The first involved a young lad called Ricky Royle. His body had been found drowned in the River Thames. The conclusion of the official police investigation was that he'd fallen in the water, but his family were never prepared to accept that. So along with my fellow psychic mediums and co-stars in the series, TJ Higgs and Tony Stockwell, I conducted an investigation which highlighted things that possibly the police should have taken a closer look at.

As we began our investigation, the police made it clear that they didn't approve. At one point the producer of the show was called in to see an irate senior police officer and was told—in no uncertain terms—not to pursue this. He replied in equally plain language that we live in a free country and we were going to pursue whatever avenues of inquiry we felt it right to explore.

I soon understood why they were so keen for us to back off.

I was able to make contact with Ricky. His energy was high. He was, understandably, angry about what had happened to him and the fact that justice had not been done. During the course of the connection, he showed me a black car, with a group of youths inside. He then showed me that on

209

the night of his death he had been involved in an altercation with the youths. There seemed to be a racist overtone to it. They had begun shouting abuse at him and he had retaliated. What had begun as an argument quickly escalated into a violent brawl.

I saw quite clearly that the youths in the car had brutally beaten him up. He had received blows to the head which had killed him. In a panic, the youths had bundled Ricky into the back of this car, driven a short distance to the Thames and dumped his body in the river.

Afterwards a member of Ricky's family told me that a black BMW had been caught on CCTV on the night of his alleged accidental death. But the police had ignored it, thinking that it had no value as evidence. The family had always believed that it had.

There were many anomalies in the case. For instance, Ricky was terrified of water and his family were adamant that he would not have gone down to the river.

On top of this, the police surmised that he'd gone down to the river to relieve himself. But the coroner's report showed that he had an empty bladder. It didn't add up.

It's always frustrating when police ignore what seems to be perfectly good evidence. But ultimately you have to accept that it isn't the psychic's place to solve the crime. That's the police's job. Our agenda is to relieve the suffering of the family, particularly that of the mother and father.

In this case, I hope we achieved that. By showing that Ricky's spirit had carried on and was capable

210

of communicating his thoughts and his feelings and his emotions and memories, maybe that gave them the strength to carry on fighting to get justice for him.

SPIRIT SECRET
Compassion enables, sympathy disables.

Shots In The Dark

The other case that always sticks in my mind was the one in which we did an investigation into what really happened at the infamous Deepcut Army Barracks.

Deepcut was an Army Barracks near Camberley in Surrey where in the space of seven years, between 1995 and 2002, no less than four trainees had been found dead. In each case they had been recorded as suicides by the coroners' courts, despite the overwhelming evidence to the contrary. One of the young privates had been found dead with five bullet wounds to his chest, for instance. Another had two bullet holes in his head.

The deaths became a big media story when the families came forward to publicly say they didn't believe the verdicts of the coroners. An official inquiry was launched into what went on there, but again the families regarded it as a whitewash. The initial investigations were carried out by Surrey Police, who discovered that there were all sorts of problems at the barracks—there was low morale, unsupervised access to weapons, bullying and the handing out of 'informal sanctions'.

As part of the series *Psychic Private Eyes* we were asked to go along and investigate the case. Myself and two of my fellow psychic mediums,

TJ Higgs and Tony Stockwell, were taken to Surrey and asked to pick up on anything we could find psychically or mediumistically.

It wasn't an easy investigation to conduct. The Ministry of Defence made it absolutely plain that there was no way we were going to be allowed anywhere near the barracks. We weren't even going to be allowed on the vast site.

Deepcut is set in open countryside and is surrounded by woodland and a public footpath. Even then, however, the MoD weren't very happy that we were in the vicinity.

Now, it may be purely coincidental but on the night when TJ Higgs and I were asked to do some night filming on a public footpath that runs along the edge of the barracks, the path was mysteriously closed off to the public. Someone from the film crew had been down there to do a recce earlier in the day and the path was open. But when darkness fell and we went down, there was an MoD sign saying 'closed due to danger to the public'.

It was dark and we were working with night vision cameras. Every now and again something odd would happen. We had joggers suddenly emerging out of dark woods and trying to barge past us on the footpath; all sorts of things happened. It was soon pretty clear to everyone that the MoD was trying to spook us.

Nevertheless, by moving around the perimeter of the camp we were able to pick up quite a bit of useful information. And as we did so, it became clear why the MoD were so keen to keep a lid on things. The circumstances surrounding the alleged suicide of the lad that we were asked to investigate had elements of impossibility about it. He couldn't possibly have inflicted the wounds he'd sustained on himself.

The spirit connections were very strong and we soon had a description of an individual and a name. When we mentioned this name to people in the know, TJ and I were told in no uncertain terms that 'it would be best if you never said anything about this'.

We couldn't broadcast the details and I am still not at liberty to reveal them because they would get me into a lot of trouble. But it was someone in a senior position connected to the MoD.

For me, however, the most revealing evidence came from one of the four young trainees. During the filming, I made contact with him and he communicated with me what had really happened there. Because it is still such a sensitive case, I have to be incredibly careful about what I say.

The boy had been traumatised by what had happened to him. As a result, as can be the case when someone has left this life in violent circumstances, his transition to the other side had not been an easy one. But he was pleased that his parents and friends had worked so hard to have the truth brought out. He asked me to pass that message on to his family, which I did.

He then showed me, in quite graphic detail, some images from the night he died. Out of discretion, I have to keep them to myself. The only thing I can say is that he did not commit suicide.

Again, it wasn't my job to publicly expose what had been going on inside Deepcut. The families and indeed the media were doing that job very effectively. Nor was it my place to bring the people responsible for whatever occurred there to justice.

I am a medium, not a lawyer or a police officer.

As a medium, however, I once more felt a sense of some satisfaction. As in the case of Ricky Royle, I believe I helped some of the victims' parents reach a clearer understanding of what had happened so that they could move on with their lives. In the end, they were vindicated by a court.

Eventually, in May 2009, an inquiry recorded a new 'open verdict' on the case.

Thankfully Deepcut Barracks has now been closed down so the tragedies that happened at that particular establishment won't happen again. The memories of what happened there, however, will live on for a very long time indeed.

'Death is not extinguishing the light; it is putting out the lamp because dawn has come.'
RABINDRANATH TAGORE

The Other Side Of The Fence

I was on tour in Dublin when someone from the television production company handed me a plain, A4 manila envelope. 'Please don't open the envelope, but please tell us what you sense,' she said.

The moment I picked it up my head was filled with a powerful and sinister mixture of images. 'This is about a young girl who was murdered,' I said. 'And I can see this man who watched her from a place at the end of her road.'

The production assistant simply nodded and said thank you. 'I can't tell you any more than that at the moment, Colin, sorry. It's to do with a psychic investigation we may want you to take part in back in London,' she said before heading off.

This wasn't unusual on the *Psychic Private Eyes* production. Myself and my fellow mediums TJ Higgs and Tony Stockwell were always kept in the dark about the cases we were to be given. It helped ensure the evidence we produced was spontaneous rather than stagemanaging our readings—which never worked.

I was intrigued by the envelope but soon forgot all about it.

It was a few weeks later that I was asked whether I would go and meet a lady called Linda Bowman. She had apparently written to me via the production company. The envelope I had been shown in Dublin contained information that she had given the team. I was told that she was the mother of a girl called Sally Anne Bowman whose murder had been featured quite prominently in the media in the preceding months.

Sally Anne Bowman was a pretty south London teenager with an exciting life in front of her. She had attended the famous BRIT school and was just starting a career as a model when she was brutally murdered, stabbed and then raped near her home in Croydon in September 2005, just two weeks after her eighteenth birthday.

I have to say actually, I had only vaguely heard of the case. I remember catching it on the news and thinking, 'Oh God, that's the area where my niece lives,' but I had thought no more about it. It's an awful thing to say, but I just put it down as another one of those awful crimes that you hear on the news. For me, however, it soon became much more than that.

I began working on the case before going to see Linda Bowman. Along with TJ Higgs and Tony

Stockwell I began working psychically on the information we'd been given.

I kept seeing this place, a refuse or recycling plant; I saw a chained fence. I didn't understand it at this point, but was confident it would make sense eventually.

At this point the police investigation still hadn't apprehended Sally Anne's killer. I was getting the strong feeling that it was connected to this fence. As when I'd first held the envelope in Dublin, I sensed someone watching Sally Anne, waiting to pounce.

Eventually it was arranged for me to go and see Linda at her home in south London. She'd specifically asked for me to go.

The moment I arrived I knew that I was tapping into some powerful energy.

At the bottom of the cul de sac where Linda lived there was a recycling plant with a chain-link fence. It was just as I'd seen earlier. I had a very strong sense that her attacker had not necessarily worked here, but that he'd worked in a place like this.

At the house I met the Bowman family. They were—and are—a wonderful, strong collection of individuals. Gathered in the house that day were Linda, Sally Anne's three sisters and Sally Anne's boyfriend, the poor lad who had been at one time a suspect.

They asked me if I was willing to do a reading, which I was. It was very emotional from the outset.

Sally Anne came through very quickly indeed; it was as if she was close by, simply waiting for someone to connect with her. They knew it was her from the very beginning. It was initially just

216

Sally Anne connecting and giving them happy memories and positive thoughts. It was so emotional, it was one of those encounters where I was affected by the tragedy of it and my feelings for the family.

I had liked and empathised with Linda and her family from the moment I met them so I was pleased to be helping them with the reading. Strangely, Sally Anne had been a big fan and, although she was a young woman, she had told her mother that if she died she would come back through me.

But as it went on I began to sense other, darker information being passed on by Sally Anne, much of which I can't repeat.

A police liaison officer had come to the house with me. The reading was being filmed by the production company. In an adjoining room the liaison officer was watching it on a monitor with the producer. Apparently the officer had been shocked at the detailed information I produced during the reading. According to the producer she turned to her at one point and said, 'How the f*** does he know that?'

We've never released some of the information into the public domain. Some of it confirmed the connection to a place with a chain-link fence outside. Even though a lot of it was shown on television, there were other things that I asked them not to include in the programme and which will remain private and confidential. As far as I was concerned, that section of the reading was for Linda and her family alone.

From the investigation's point of view, myself, TJ Higgs and Tony Stockwell produced lots of relevant and important information.

We came up with a name, Mark. We came up with the fact he'd been in Australia and had attacked other women.

There were connections to the place where she was attacked. He was older than the people he hung around with. He worked in catering. We came up with so many pieces of information.

It took a long time but eventually the police got there.

In February 2008 Mark Dixie was tried and found guilty of Sally Anne's murder and sentenced to life imprisonment. In court it was revealed that Dixie was a serial sex offender with a long history of harassing women. The policeman in charge of the case called for a national DNA register. He claimed it would have enabled them to apprehend Mark Dixie within twenty-four hours.

I have remained on good terms with the Bowman family since then and have been in contact with Linda Bowman on several occasions. They are now getting on with their lives but they will never forget Sally Anne. I am pleased to have played a very small part in helping them achieve some sort of peace.

A Bucketful Of Money

As a psychic medium, I am constantly receiving the most unusual and sometimes bizarre requests.

Some of them are harmless. For instance, I get asked to find missing cats and dogs all the time. I always decline politely. It's not that I'm unsympathetic. I am a dog lover myself. But I always explain that it's simply not what I do.

At other times I am asked to find things that have gone missing, like wedding or engagement rings. Again, I say no as diplomatically as I can.

I'm not always quite so delicate in my replies. Once a woman wrote to me, asking me to use my psychic ability to tell her whether her husband was having an affair with her sister. There are some areas of people's private lives with which I don't want to get involved. So I wrote back to her and told her I sympathised with her marital problems but that my name was Colin Fry, not Jeremy Kyle. Unsurprisingly, I never heard from her again.

Over the years, however, I have agreed to take on a number of unusual investigations. Some of the most intriguing have been connected to the business and financial world.

One of the first of these cases came about several years ago when I was introduced at a party to a gentleman named Peter, a seemingly very successful international businessman. To my surprise he was interested in and pretty well informed about the subject of spiritualism and mediumship. I already had a fairly good reputation at that point and was particularly known for my trance sittings, where Magnus often came through. Peter had heard about this and said he was interested in having a reading. In particular he was interested in talking to Magnus.

I didn't ask him whether he had a particular reason for wanting to speak to him. I simply agreed to a trance reading and fixed a date with him.

Of course when I'm in a trance, I am oblivious to whatever it is Magnus talks to people about. So I have to rely on what Peter said and the tapes that he made. (As it happens, at the time when this took place people were still allowed to make tape recordings of their readings with me. Now, for legal reasons, they are not.)

It turned out that Peter had invested a very large amount of money in what were supposed to have been United States Government bonds. He did so as part of a syndicate of wealthy businessmen. This was during the first Bush administration in the early 1990s. Then the money went missing and the American authorities denied all knowledge of it.

Peter had a series of sittings with Magnus, who said that he wasn't usually interested in the financial affairs of people on this side of life. However, in this particular instance there was a case of great wrongdoing. So he started giving Peter insight into how this international syndicate could prove that the money had been stolen from them by the US Government.

Peter seemed to be very pleased about this and said he'd be back in contact with me again. Sure enough he called a few weeks later and arranged for me to fly out to Switzerland.

I boarded a plane a few days later and was whisked off to an office block, where I met the other members of Peter's syndicate. I performed another trance reading with Magnus on their behalf in which, apparently, Magnus confirmed what he'd told Peter.

Frustratingly it was one of those cases in which I didn't get to hear the final outcome. I got the strong sense, however, that it had been successful. There were two reasons for thinking this. Firstly I got the distinct impression that Peter was going to use the information he'd got through Magnus to begin a legal case. This was, undoubtedly, going to take many, many years of legal wrangling.

The main reason I sensed it had gone well, however, was the phone call I received not long afterwards.

'Are you Colin Fry the medium?' the voice asked.

'Yes.'

'I have got rather a strange assignment and I was wondering whether you'd be interested. I'd like you to come and sit and look at someone.'

'What?'

'Look at someone. And then tell me what you think of him.'

I was quite well known within the spiritualist movement but I had no idea how they had heard of me in the City.

The man offered to pay me quite generously but I was also intrigued. What could they possibly want me to tell them by looking at someone? So I agreed to travel up to London and met my contact at the company's headquarters. I can't identify the company for reasons of confidentiality.

We sat down in his office and he explained that I wasn't going to meet the person in question directly. I was simply going to observe him from a distance. 'I just want you to tell me whatever it is you sense or pick up about this person,' the man said. 'Anything at all you detect, please tell me.'

The offices were mainly open plan with the rooms divided by glass, so you could see into every working area of the building. I was taken to a small room with a comfortable chair and a desk. Adjacent to this room was a much bigger, boardroom-type space, where there were a large number of people gathering for a meeting.

I had been asked to observe the man who was making a presentation at the meeting.

As this meeting got under way I sat there drinking a coffee, trying to look inconspicuous and as if I was waiting for an interview or a meeting. I couldn't hear the conversation, but I saw one man rise to his feet and begin to make a presentation to what looked like a board of directors. He was an ordinary-looking guy, probably in his late twenties to early thirties. There was nothing about him that struck me immediately.

The board members all seemed quite happy with him, apart from my contact, the man who had asked me to do this. He looked uncomfortable and twitchy and was deliberately not looking in my direction.

At that point I realised that what he was doing wasn't official. I realised that he was acting independently, and I suspected it was because he had some kind of private concerns about the guy making the presentation.

The spirit world can communicate with us in the most unexpected and sometimes creative ways. I often find myself receiving information completely out of the blue. I won't be aware that a particular spirit is present. All that will happen is that suddenly I will have a thought or an image placed in my mind. It is then up to me to understand and interpret it. That's precisely what happened here.

At first, as I watched the men and women in the room deep in discussion, I didn't really detect anything. But then, a few minutes into the meeting, my head was filled with a single image. It was so clear I can still see it now. It was of a bucket full of money, banknotes, which was being emptied down a drain.

As the meeting continued I received very little else. At one point I sensed someone telling me, 'He is not a bad man, he's simply doing what he's paid to do.'

I sat there for about twenty-five minutes in all. When the meeting drew to a close the guy I'd been briefed by returned and asked me what I thought.

'All I can say is based on what I sensed,' I said. 'But I got the very strong feeling that the man I was observing is involved in a huge international fraud.'

I remember the shocked expression on the man's face. 'What do you mean? How do you know this?' he asked.

'I don't know what this man's role is within your company but he has been put in a position of huge trust,' I said. 'He's not a bad person. But he is basically going too far in doing what he's doing. And you are going to lose millions and millions of pounds over it.'

'Oh God no,' he kept saying.

A few moments later I left the building and headed home. I thought nothing more of it until six months later when I was watching the evening news.

The newsreader mentioned the name of the financial institution I'd visited and explained that it was at the centre of a huge, international financial fraud. The next thing I saw was a picture of a man—the one I'd seen in the meeting room in the City months earlier.

As the report continued, it emerged that he had been given way too much responsibility and had been fraudulently trading in stocks and shares to the tune of many millions of pounds.

The fraud he'd committed went on to dominate the news headline for weeks and months afterwards. In the end his actions destroyed the financial institution, one of the oldest and most respected in the City of London.

If one image summed up the entire story it was the one that the spirit world flashed into my head: a bucket full of money being poured down a drain.

A Number On The Door

People often ask me whether the spirit world is a harmonious and peaceful place. The answer is a resounding yes. And the reason for this is that the spirit dimension is free from the one thing that is at the root of so many of the conflicts and injustices on this earthly plane: fear.

The spirit world has frequently shown me how fear holds so many people back, how it allows the negative to overshadow the positive in life. It also sometimes allows the evil in our world to dominate the good.

My communications with the spirit world regularly show me the importance of overcoming fear. It was never more clearly illustrated than when I did a demonstration at the Alexandra Theatre in Birmingham a couple of years ago.

I was coming to the end of the demonstration when I felt myself in the presence of a young, black guy. He was directing me towards his brother who was in the audience.

I felt a real anger in the spirit I was connected to; he was giving me the real impression that he had been at the centre of a terrible injustice.

The young man in the audience was with his sisters. They had come along together in the hope of making contact with their brother.

As the message went on they explained that their brother had been murdered in cold blood somewhere in the city. No one had ever been charged with the crime.

They were, of course, desperate to know that he had made it safely to the other side. And they were very emotional when I was able to reassure them that he had. But it was the second part of the message that really shook them.

As the boy continued to connect with me, I was also shown images of a particular area in Birmingham. I reeled off a number of street names and eventually settled on one particular street. As I described it there were murmurs around the theatre. It was clear people knew where I was talking about. It was also clear that this was an area with a notorious reputation. It was not somewhere people would choose to go.

As the message continued I was shown a house. I was then shown the house number and a flat number inside the house.

'Please tell the police that if they want to find out who murdered your brother, they should make enquiries at this address,' I said.

And I remember the audience were all in hushed silence. There was no applause. I think people were too shocked. I also sensed that a lot of people were also a little bit fearful.

One of the frustrations of my job is that I often don't get to hear what happens to people after they have received a message from me. The young man and his sisters didn't stop to talk to me after the show. I was quite keen to talk to them because I had felt uneasy about giving out the details. But I had seen them heading off into the night before I could reach them.

It was several months later that I got a letter postmarked from Birmingham. It was a very formal letter and it read:

Dear Mr Fry,
My sisters and I felt that we should write to you. We had to think long and hard about whether we should go to the police with the information you gave us at the theatre that night. If we are honest we were a bit afraid. We thought they would laugh at us when we told them how we'd got the address you gave us.

But in the end we thought about what you said about not being frightened and we did go along to the police station.

The police did act on the information and they went along to the flat at the address you gave us where they spoke to some people who they hadn't spoken to before. It seems they knew something about our brother's murder.

The police have told us that they are now pursuing a lead that they believe will now help them to catch our brother's killer.

We can't thank you enough for what you have done.

The letter affected me deeply on several levels. To begin with it was incredibly gratifying to know that I'd been helpful in—perhaps—bringing to justice someone who had so far evaded the law. But it was also a reminder of how important it was that I

226

trusted my instincts when channelling and passing on messages from the other side.

I remember coming off stage that night and saying to a member of my crew, 'I'm not sure if I should have given that message.'

The crew member said, 'If that's what you are being shown then you had to'.

And he was quite right. There are times when the information I am given is so important that I can't hold it back. Sometimes the truth has to come out.

CONCLUSION

'You live on earth only for a few short years, which you call an incarnation, and then you leave your body as an outworn dress and go for refreshment to your true home in the spirit.' WHITE EAGLE

Doing A Deal With Angels

Many people seem to think that the spirit world controls my life. On more than one occasion someone has come up to me and said: 'Oh, Colin, you are so lucky. It must be wonderful to have all these guides who can steer you through life and tell you what to do.'

They look quite shocked when I say to them: 'Do you actually think that I take that much notice of them, that I live by every utterance they make to me?'

Why on earth would I let a spirit guide have control of my life? I don't do everything they say, I don't agree with every observation they make, but there is an understanding between us. And I do listen to the guidance they give. It's then down to me to choose whether to act upon it.

I believe that thanks to their guidance I have been led to places and situations where there has been knowledge which I have then picked up. But I have always picked that knowledge up of my own free will. That's the difference.

It's the difference between being shown a path and choosing to walk down that path.

Sometimes I think it's as if they've had me on a forty-seven-and-a-half year treasure hunt. And it's been fun and sometimes it's been difficult. But then it wouldn't be fun if it wasn't difficult.

It's a life that constantly throws up its surprises and pleasures. Recently, for instance, I spent some time with the comedian Freddie Starr. We got on very well, partly because we found we had a lot in common.

He says that to be a successful comedian you make a pact with the devil of comedy who says you can be successful and have audiences of 2,000 people but the price is you must always be funny.

I have signed a similar pact, except in my case it's a deal with the angels.

I have this unwritten contract with the angels that says they will let me do what I want in life, they will help me heal people and my life will be successful. But there's a price I have to pay and I have to pay it willingly. And that price is that I have to give back.

In order to have this happy and positive life, the price is that I have to live a life of service.

The good news is that I don't have an issue with that. I'd rather have a life of service than one in which I was locked away like a hermit.

I remember once Magnus said to me that there have been many great people through the course of history who locked themselves away and attained knowledge but that it was wasted because although they learned a great deal they never went out and shared it with the world.

I don't intend to do that. And I hope this book has helped share some of the wisdom that I have acquired so far in my life.

'Humans are amphibians—half spirit and half animal. As spirits they belong to the eternal world, but as animals they inhabit time.' C.S. LEWIS

The Christening Robe

As I said at the beginning of this book, the spirit world is a vast network of contacts, all ready, willing and able to help each of us get through our lives here on this earthly plane.

One day, of course, those of us who are currently living this existence will pass over and join them. We will simply be continuing a process that is as old as time itself.

Our places here will be taken by others who will in time be replaced by others, and so it will go on. Life keeps regenerating itself, both on this and the other side.

With this thought in mind I will end with one final story. It actually echoes one of the stories with which I began, the story of Maria, the lady who travelled from Brazil to receive a message from her grandfather predicting that she was going to adopt a baby.

It's funny sometimes how messages repeat themselves, because not very long after I received that message, I received another, very similar one. In this particular case it wasn't at a private reading but at a demonstration at a theatre in East Anglia.

It didn't begin too promisingly. All I heard at first was a name resonating in my head: Pongo.

At first, I really didn't know how to react. It was such a rude name. I certainly didn't imagine someone would shoot their hand into the air and identify themselves in the packed ranks of the theatre's dress circle. And I certainly didn't expect that hand to belong to a rather well-turned-out, thirty-something lady.

'Pongo was my favourite stuffed animal toy when I was a child,' she explained.

'My love, I have a lady with me who is telling me her name is Eileen. She's a real character,' I said.

'That sounds like my grandmother.'

'She knows you've been a bad girl,' I continued, drawing an embarrassed look from her. 'You've spent three hundred pounds that you weren't supposed to spend.'

Her husband was sitting next to her. To judge by the look on her face, she wished that the earth would open up and swallow her.

But the message soon took a different direction. 'She wants to say that she has loved being around you the last three months,' I told the lady.

She didn't really react to this.

'She also wants to say that there is a christening robe, made out of an old wedding dress or the veil of an old wedding dress, that the family has kept,' I said.

The lady wasn't sure at first what this meant. But then her husband whispered something to her.

'Oh yes, I know,' she said.

'My love, your gran is telling me that she thinks it should have another airing.'

At this the lady's face became much more serious.

'My husband and I can't have children,' she said.

But I got the very strong sense that that was not what Eileen meant. I was reminded of the feelings

I'd got when I'd relayed the message from Maria's grandfather. I felt, once more, that the spirit wasn't talking about having a new baby.

So at that point I actually told the lady the story of Maria travelling from Brazil to see me. As I approached the end of the story, and the moment when the nun unexpectedly arrived at her front door looking for a home for a beautiful little boy, I saw her face changing. A penny had dropped and soon her face was wreathed in the most beatific smile.

'We've actually just adopted a baby in the last three months,' she said, beaming now.

The audience erupted into huge applause.

'That's what she meant when she said she had been enjoying watching you these last three months,' I said.

'That's wonderful to know, Colin,' the lady said, crying now. 'She loved babies and she'd have loved to have met our new baby.'

'Well she has met her,' I confirmed. 'And she'll continue to watch over her always.'

In that sense it was a perfect message, one that sums up all that I have described in this book. For this family, their story was moving on. A new generation was joining the family; the circle of life here on this earthly plane was turning once more. But, as this message illustrates so well, the family network was still alive in the spirit dimension as well. The lady's grandmother was very much there. She wasn't the hands-on influence for the baby and her mother that she would have been if she'd remained in this life, but her warmth, wisdom and presence were still there to be felt and drawn upon nevertheless.

The life we lead on this earthly plane is only a part of our existence. It continues on the other side. We cannot see it, but the two worlds run in parallel. They are inter-connected and there are times when we are extremely close, much closer than we can imagine.

The spirits of those who have left us here in this life are still close at hand, watching over us. This is the way it has always worked—and always will work. It will be this way in the next generation and the generation after that.

We are all connected. We are all living side by side.